Horus Templar

and the

Case of the Jolly Jaywalker

E.L. WARD

Horus Templar and the Case of the Jolly Jaywalker is a work of fiction. Names, characters, places, and incidents either are the product of the author's imagination or are used fictitiously. Any resemblance to actual persons, living or dead, events, or locales is entirely coincidental.

ISBN: 978-1-7370436-5-2

Shoeprint image on cover licensed from Furtseff via Depositphotos.com

Table of Contents

"Everything apparently 'good' about you is the fruit of meticulous conditioning. You should live in dread of the man you would be, had we not taken great pains to impose someone else on you."

- Magormissahr, *Referendums on the World, Vol. 412*

Chapter 1

It was getting so he hardly recognized the place.

Sergeant Basil waded into the light of another warm-glowing egress window, faintly registering the scuff of his own freshly-polished shoes, or the gentle rap of his nightstick as he absently tapped it against his shoulder, letting his eyes rove around an alleyway that was now practically alien to him. Of course, some changes had seemed gradual enough across his many years of nightly patrols. By this time, he'd already become well-accustomed to the renovated stoop in front of the miller's place, and most of the manholes from the ongoing expansion of the sewer system – fairly harmless alterations, in and of themselves. Really, it was something about the general character of the burg after dark that he couldn't seem to get used to. The chill was taken out of the stoney walls by the steadily-multiplying streetlamps. The droning bustle of the daylight hours kept intruding into later and later watches, and the pathways he remembered as barren and inert were suddenly burdened with a steady trickle of people from dusk till dawn. The restless life of the inner city was pushing its way ever further outward. Even now, he passed by a family with three small children, feeling a pang of anxiety as he watched their little faces lean dangerously close to the picture window of a shop filled with confections. A shop that, only yesterday, it seemed, he didn't even know was a bakery. A shop that had always been closed long before he passed it by, and had therefore been invisible. But not anymore. Now there were young people breathing on its glass, and Basil was forced to wonder if they understood the gravity of their situation, should they reach out just a few inches more and actually *touch* it. He could let them off with a warning, of course. And he would, unquestionably. But that was rather beside the point. Unavoidably, the more sleepless a city became, the more apt it was to get into trouble.

Soon after he left the bakery behind – thankfully, without incident – Sergeant Basil came to yet another strange new feature of the night: a fellow officer. In what he had by now unconsciously deemed 'the good old days,' this was perhaps the last thing Basil would've ever found on his patrol. At first, it'd been enough to split his original route up between two cops... then three. But by this time, he wasn't just walking his own, smaller circuit. Now, there was overlap.

"Evening, Basil," his counterpart was the first to hail.

"Good evening, Mr. Turmeric," Basil replied, deftly tipping his bobby with the end of his nightstick. He didn't yet know Turmeric well, but he had a good feeling they were kindred spirits, both being men of few words, and perhaps equally unenthused at finding themselves in a position to exchange them now. It also helped that they were both Sergeants, as all men with seasonings for names were required to be.

The two men drew back under the deep shadow of a nearby wall, dutifully surveilling in silence, having already exhausted all they wished to say. "A bit on the warm side," Basil offered anyway.

"Yes, a bit," Turmeric agreed, airing out his leather gloves by pure reflex, as if this was the first he'd noticed.

For a while after, silence ensued. But then, inevitably, Turmeric cleared his throat, heralding *the question*...

"Has there been any excitement?"

Basil let out a slow breath. It didn't matter if Turmeric was obliged to check in as a responsible officer. They both knew his *real* reason for asking superseded any point of procedure. Anyway, the quiet, artificial nonchalance of his voice betrayed his anxiety, to say nothing of the irrational idea that he would ever have to ask in the first place. As if Basil would've held back about any brushes with *him*... the emergent terror of St. Argonsburg...

"No," he answered. And that might've been the end of it, had he not found himself overcome with the same irrational curiosity. "You?"

"No," Turmeric replied. "Another quiet night, so far."

Basil nodded, electing to resume his route. "Quiet, yes," he sighed. "But never so quiet as it used to be."

* * *

"Where did you say? 'Carnivore Avenue'?" Basil asked, stroking his chin – making what conspicuous signs he could of genuine confoundedness, so as not to seem mistrusting.

"Y...yea," the poor fellow confirmed, still horribly afraid. "Verily it was told unto me that I would'st find it betwixt Spruce Street and Evergreen Lane. But I hath searched out Evergreen Lane from first to last, and ne'er were such roads to be found!"

Basil suppressed a sigh. Small wonder the young man was lost. He was almost certainly another recent transplant from out-of-town. Not only did his high grammar ring a bit off-key, but the very fact that he chose to employ it placed him outside Deputy Constable Miloje's jurisdiction, where plainspokenness was understood to be preferred. But at least his problem turned out to be something the sergeant could remedy. "My lad, I'm sure you must mean *Conifer* Avenue. And I'm afraid it's not to be found in the city proper. It's within a stone's throw of the Harbor." He stepped aside, gesturing down the way and around a bend to the left. "If you go down to Messidor Alley and follow it clear out of town, you'll eventually come to another stretch of Evergreen Lane. Conifer will be just beyond that."

The man's face brightened with breathless exuberance. "Oh, thank you, Sir! Thank you! I twas hopeless to findeth my way! I shalt forever be in thy debt!"

"Think nothing of it, Lad," Basil assured him. "Best of luck in your new vocation. Eh, what line of work did you say you'd been conscripted to?"

"Ship's navigator, Sir."

"Ah, but of course. The *very* best of luck to you indeed. And might I also suggest the timely purchase of a compass?"

The young man laughed a nervous laugh, even as he began to back away excitedly down the sidewalk. "Yes, Sir! A fine suggestion, Sir! I shan't disappoint you!"

Basil only nodded. It wasn't until the fellow was quite far off that he finally released his sigh, turning and beginning to wade back up the side of the street, while another whole posse of potential interactions parted ways around him. This had to be the busiest he'd ever seen Kobayashi Street, so late at night. A hasty survey of his surroundings tallied another three groups of people approaching on his side of the road, two more travelling on ahead, a steady trickle of folks on the other side, and even one in crossing at the shelf in the hill.

Just as he came up alongside Nonstarter Parkway, the voices of several more people sprung out to meet him. He paused a moment at the sudden noise and searched down the side street, weighing whether what he heard was loud and rude enough to call for his attention, or simply a trick of the acoustics...

But just then, out of nowhere, a distant call rang out from the shelf above – a cry of distress. "Stop! Stop him! Police! It's him! It's *him*!"

Basil whirled back, his eyes searching through time as well as space. The survey he took – the lone man crossing the street. Could it be? Without even realizing it, had he really just witnessed...?

He didn't wait to finish the question. Darting for the crosswalk at the top of the slope, he knew the answer would be there waiting for him, if it was true. His surety only grew as he traced a trail of fresh prints on the street, listing to the left. Even so, his throat stopped up when he saw it. There, on the stone just to the left of the crosswalk line, in the pallid light of an Other World, he found the mark – the signature – the calling card. The small, muddy shoeprint that had lately stalked the nightmares of every cop in St. Argonsburg, manifested on the ground right before his eyes. Though it was a warm night, the next breath he took froze his blood. For a moment, all he could do was stand in place – his jaw working, but both word and deed escaping him. And he remained stuck that way until the call rang out again...

"Stop him! He's getting away!"

Basil leapt back into pursuit, if only by reflex. He flew across the walk, only to stop again and despair when he reached the other side. Where was he supposed to go? The villain could've fled down any of several alleys near at hand. Which did he choose? Why were there no more prints to show him the way? He could feel the perpetrator doubling and tripling his lead by the moment, and it only served to make his choice that much more impossible...

"Over there!" the same caller instructed him. Basil's eyes finally spied the source: a man pointing emphatically by the roadside. "He went that way!"

Once again, Basil found himself on the chase. He barreled down the alleyway, fumbling his whistle up to his lips. He blew so hard that the cork ball only rattled. He tried again and finally got a few good blasts off. He ran for all he was worth. But the pools of light ahead of him were all empty, as far as he could see. Squinting as he passed under each lamp, he could only sound his whistle again and again, hoping against hope that it would miraculously conjure another officer in the fiend's way...

Finally, he was drawing up on an intersection – another small alley running in traverse. Three ways to go, and this time, no one to point out the right one. But even as he ground to a halt before the crossroads – the despair of indecision constricting him tightly – he heard a faint groan. His eyes flicked to his left, and there he found a man splayed out on the ground, clutching his eye. Over top of him, a sign post wiggled and teetered on the ends of its chains. Basil only watched as a small trickle of blood ran under the man's hand...

Dazed, the fellow slowly blinked, his one exposed eye wandering through the skies, fixing on nothing particular. Until, at last, he found the sergeant standing over him. His mouth worked to form words, as his free hand pointed shakily up the lane.

"He... he went..."

Now, of course, this was the feeble start of an accusation that Basil had to consider with all possible reservation. Any criminal – caught in flight – might try to pass himself off as a bowled-over bystander, if left with no other recourse. But by this time, Basil was already busy forming his assessment. He eyed the man's shoes, finding them to be quite the wrong size – and with no great abundance of mud caked into the left sole. Yes, from all he could gather, this was an earnest tip. He crouched down by the man. "You saw him?"

"I..." the man said weakly, his eye fluttering. He rested flat on the ground.

Just before Basil might've sprung back up, he heard rapid footfalls coming up behind him. He turned to meet none other than Sergeant Turmeric.

"What's happened?" he asked. "Surely not...?"

"Yes, I'm afraid so," Basil interjected, pointing. "After him! I'm going to stay with the witness."

"Of course." Turmeric nodded and hopped back into full pursuit. His whistle blared a moment later, and Basil began to hear its call recited back to him from far off. The restless night air filled with fast-spreading alarm. Officers from all over the district would soon be converging on his haunt. Even so, Basil feared the chase was already a lost cause. It would be nothing to slip back into the streams of commuters and disappear. No... the only real prize in all this was what he had right in front of him. He reached out, giving the man's shoulder a gentle shake.

"Wake up, son," Basil almost whispered. "You must tell me what happened."

The man came around blearily. "He... ran into me. Threw me down..."

"Did you get a good look at him?"

He only breathed for a while. "I... I'm not sure I..."

"Lad, you must tell me everything. Who is he? This man, Lazarus?"

Chapter 2

FREE-DOME!

Horus could only wince at the newspaper in his hand, studying the oversized front-page story with complete incomprehension. He ruffled the paper once against the imaginary breeze, as if it would help him read the bold script any better under the warm, bright light of day. He even tried canting the paper off to one side. But of course, none of it proved the least bit enlightening. He sat blankly on the city bench, finding himself in the most unusual fix of wishing the news story had some context, or even a little content...

...When suddenly, he was joined by a Human on his left, whose old bones groaned as he plopped down onto the far end of the bench. Horus snuck a glance at the elderly man with the long, grey beard, trying to gauge whether he might want to be bothered with a bit of small talk. After all, men of his age usually had some awareness of the latest gossip – or, failing knowledge, at least an opinion. But watching his thick spectacles scan the busy sidewalk, Horus quickly decided the old fellow would probably prefer to be left to his thoughts. Even so, after a moment more of having not the faintest idea what he was pretending to read, Horus changed his mind, resolving to venture the question anyway...

"..." Horus went to say, folding his paper down, when the man abruptly cut him off...

"Well, look whose broken-down old butt finally managed to drag itself outta bed this mornin'," the Greybeard said.

Horus was momentarily dumbstruck, until he noticed that the man was addressing a second fellow on a slow approach... practically identical in age, posture, stigmatism, dental decline, and of course, facial hair.

"Ha! 'Finally,' he says," the second Greybeard laughed sardonically. "Who do ya think you're foolin', anyway? As if I didn't see your rickety chicken-legs fold under that bench just a couple seconds ago." With familiar effort, he sat down at the far *right* side of the bench, prompting Horus – who was in the middle – to politely retreat to his paper.

"Not so spry yourself, there, Champ," Greybeard #1 quipped.

"What can I say? Gout is Heck."

"Don't I know it."

Having reached an agreement, the two men synchronously unrolled newspapers of their own. Seeing he was in amicable company – at least equally concerned with current events – Horus politely gave them a minute to consider the headlines, with the resolution to engage them both, as soon as it seemed appropriate. But just as he was opening his mouth a second time, he was interrupted again...

"My, my, my..." Greybeard #2 tsked, shaking his head at the front page. "Now there's a fine mess for ya, and no mistake. I never thought I'd see the day."

"Shameful," Greybeard #1 commiserated. "Just shameful..."

Horus grinned, seeing the chance to sate his own curiosity had been tailor-made for him. He folded his paper a second time and shifted on the bench...

"...What fine mess are we talkin' about, exactly?" Greybeard #2 asked before Horus could.

His counterpart groaned. "Don't you know nothin'? It's that Maenean insurrectionist again! 'Free-dome' - that's his catch phrase! That's the last chillin' words many-a unsuspectin' souls ever heard before he came right up and chopped 'em down. Or worse! Persuaded 'em to his evil cause!"

"Ah, I mighta knowed. How do ya figure a looney like him, gainin' traction in Maenea, of all places?"

"T'aint natural, I says," Greybeard #1 boded. "There's the old Manean proverb: 'The definition of insanity is trying somethin' new and expectin' better results.' They're the last people in the whole world oughta have any quarter fer his crazy notions: liberty... popular sovereignty. But the Countess ain't stopped him yet."

"It's the way things is headed," Greybeard #2 bemoaned, a waving finger upraised. "Take our own dear Czarina... an' her new 'Royal Comptroller'. Now there's a fella who won't rest till he's done reinvented the wheel. Wants ta change the face of the city... all in the name of '*modernity*' an' '*innovation*'. Streets ain't safe anymore with these new-fangled contraptions tearin' all around."

At that very moment, Horus chanced to see one of the very 'new-fangled contraptions' they were on about. He couldn't help a smile and a wave as a shiny, stygian double-decker bicycle passed him by. The stately lady and her husband far above returned the wave and warm expression while they both worked to power the enormous hoop-wheel at the front of the craft. It left

Horus feeling whimsically amused, even as the conversation around him poised to take an even darker caste...

"Well, there's worse things as haunt the streets these days," Greybeard #1 pointed out ominously. "But ain't no use speaking of it."

Horus' face drew back with a new dread-curiosity. He couldn't immediately call to mind any menace to the by-ways of St. Argonsburg. What were they talking about now? Or rather, what were they about to *avoid* talking about? He had to know...

"You don't mean *him*, do ya?" Greybeard #2 stifled Horus yet again. "Left-Foot Lazarus?"

Ah, yes... 'Left-Foot Lazarus' – the criminal persona of the now-infamous serial-jaywalker that had indeed gripped the city with great unrest. It was a prominent matter. But Horus was intrigued to see how it might be further embellished by a couple seasoned tellers of fish tales...

"Course I do!" Greybeard #1 scoffed. "And who else? Now there's a bogeyman an' no mistake... cut from the same cloth as Herz Bravado hisself, if y'ask me. Oh, sure... any ol' garden-variety psychopath might be capable o' jaywalkin', just fer the thrill of it... the danger... the sheer, illicit convenience. But not our Left-Foot Lazarus – oh, no. They says he leaves his mark behind him in the night... a muddy shoeprint on the cobblestone... ne'er more than a few inches beside the crosswalk!" The old fellow shivered as he painted the whole horrific scene with his words. "An' they ain't found just one footprint... nor two... nor even a dozen. Do ya *know* how many streets he done defaced by now?"

At the prompting, Horus went to venture an educated guess...

"...30!" Greybeard #1 exclaimed, having apparently intended that his question be rhetorical. "Imagine it! A 30-time offender, an' he has the audacity to rub the police's noses in it! Mark me, but that says somethin'. Says we ain't dealin' with no ordinary crook. Not hardly. This Lazarus feller be a whole new class o' criminal – a spawn of Wxldlr, ya might say. A rebel for rebellion's own sake. A man without authority!"

Greybeard #2 nodded with puffed-out lip. "Yer right on all counts, save one. Guess ya didn't see the story on page 7. Left-Foot Lazarus done crossed his 31st street last night."

Horus quickly flipped through the pages of his paper to confirm this vaguely alarming news.

"Ah, ya don't say? No chance they caught him in the act, I 'spect? He gets away squeaky clean every time..."

"Maybe not so squeaky, fer once," Greybeard #2 intoned, turning a braggart's grin nonchalantly into the distance.

Horus and Greybeard #1 looked wide-eyed down the row at him. "Whatdaya mean by that?" Greybeard #1 was the first to ask, naturally.

"They says there was collateral damage... an innocent bystander. Seems there was an officer on patrol, an' Lazarus spooked. Feller got knocked down an' busted up when he come shootin' by. Now, who knows? Maybe this feller had a good look at him before he got bowled over. Maybe the coppers'll get their first good lead in the case."

Just as Horus waxed hopeful that the SAPD might indeed be on the cusp of catching up with an admittedly singular public menace, Greybeard #1 shook his head...

"Won't matter if they got a lead or not. They'll never catch him. Law an' order just ain't what it used ta be. Ya remember a month 'r so back... they busted one-a their own Captains fer sellin' state secrets?"

"Course I do."

"Well, I don't think they caught up with themselves since."

They both put their noses back into the headline that began the whole spiel in the first place. "Yes, sirree... mayhem an' mischief on all sides," Greybeard #1 framed it. "That's what were in for."

"The times, they are a-changin'..." Greybeard #2 agreed with a tired sigh.

After just a moment or two of silent rumination by all parties, the Greybeards spontaneously commenced the painstaking effort of hauling themselves up from the bench. "Well... guess I better get on with ma day," #1 grunted.

"Yup... gotta keep movin' afore these hips lock up again," #2 answered. "See ya tomorrow. Same time, same place."

"Let's hope so."

Left suddenly to his own company, Horus grinned. "Glad we had this chat." Then, he took his turn standing up. It would seem that a case of some import might very well be taking shape. Perhaps, as one of the city's leading Public Defenders, he'd be learning quite a bit more about it in the coming days. But for the moment, he too had other places to be...

* * *

"Let's see what we have here," Horus said, drawing the brief in close with one hand as he tugged his tie loose with the other. "Bankruptcy case. Hoity

Hydroponics Research Foundation. Petitioning to reorganize." He folded the documents over to fix a questioning look on Deborah. "Alright. What's your prognosis?"

"Well, of course, a charitable organization has a busy set of books just like any commercial enterprise. But I think I've already homed in on the root of the problem," she replied airily, keeping a cool eye trained on the wall clock. "Flip to page three there; you'll find a few highlighted figures."

By reflex, Horus took a half step toward his office car's window before he caught himself, shooting a bit of a sour look over his shoulder at the stranger in the way as he pivoted into a pace in front of his desk, shuffling to the third page. "From last year's annual finance report," he announced. "Average contribution per donor per year: Forty pence and twelve shillings. Annual solicitation mailer spend per donor per year: Fifty-one thousand, three hundred eighty-seven shillings and forty-six pence." He paused a moment to stroke his jowls. "That's about standard for a charity, isn't it?"

"Yes, and they took the standard road right off the financial deep end because of it," she confirmed with an absent nod.

"I see." With a final effort, he liberated himself from his necktie, only to pick up another one from his desk, proceeding at once to fumble with both ends. "And what about their actual payout into hydroponics research? Surely that had some notable effect on their overall debt?"

Deborah shrugged. "Not really. Hydroponics has been around for decades."

"Now if we could just come up with a way to make the food grow without the water, we'd *really* have something," Gord mused as he stroked his chin, his eyes never straying from the bright vista just beyond Horus' window.

"Out of pure curiosity..." Horus began again, as he labored to form anything resembling a knot at his neck, "...do you have any notion how a foundation like this ever came about in the first place?"

"Well, you know how it is. It's all in the sales pitch. They packaged the idea as a way to spare the super-wealthy the indignity of having to eat anything that came from dirt," Deborah explained.

Horus nodded, trying to pull the end of his nail out of a loose thread. "Ah, yes. It would have to be a cause near and dear to the Czarina's own heart just to pass the board of approval."

Deborah sighed as she stood, taking her gaze down from the clock for the first time since Horus arrived. She walked right up to him and gently stole the ends of his tie. "You know, when you don't ask for help, I take that as my cue to let you handle things. But I can't just sit and watch you strangle yourself. It's kind of humiliating."

"Maybe even more humiliating than eating dirt-food," Gord posited. He snapped his fingers. "Now, there's a thought. Self-tying ties. I'll have to write that down."

"Alright – I suppose I can defer to your expertise, just this once," Horus said, grinning a bit as he surrendered any effort to tie his own tie, recalling hundreds of similar occasions in the past. Certainly, he could learn to do it himself if he wanted to. It was just the wanting to that eluded him. "It's the bow ties," he claimed. "I always have special trouble with the bow ties."

"I wouldn't know, Boss. You make them all look impossible," she quipped. "And what, pray tell, was wrong with the tie you were already wearing?"

"That was a business tie. Bows are more festive."

She raised a brow. "Oh? Is that so?"

He shrugged. "It may not be written down anywhere, but I've always thought so."

Suddenly, there was a knock on the office door.

"Perhaps that's our invite to the festivities now," Horus supposed.

Deborah deftly finished his tie in the next moment before heading to the door. She opened it with a congenial – if somewhat surprised – smile. "Oh. Hello, Blucille."

"Hello Deborah; Horus," Blucille replied as she was let in.

"Ms. Cordon," Horus greeted her, sharing Deborah's surprise. "How nice to see you. Please, have a seat."

Blucille made a quick study of the room. "I hope this isn't a bad time," she said as she sat. "That is, I was under the impression you didn't have a lot on your plate right now. But if you're busy, well..."

"Not to worry," Horus encouraged her, while Deborah returned to her own seat, and her unblinking vigil of his clock. "We were just going over the details of an upcoming bankruptcy case. Nothing that represents any present obligation. I was only mulling over whether or not to take it."

"That's something I could certainly mull over for you, if you like," Gord volunteered.

Horus' jowls contorted. He'd finally had enough of the whole gaffe. "Deborah, what is this man doing standing in my window?"

"The same thing I'm doing staring at the clock," she said. "It's all part of Royal Comptroller Sidon Thangorodrim's big push for 150 percent employment by the end of the quarter."

Horus blinked. "150 percent?"

She nodded. "That's right. Oh, I know it sounds implausible at first, but all it takes is enough people doubling-up to put the numbers over the top."

"A massive push to re-conscript the already-conscripted," Gord elaborated. "The only bear was coming up with enough extra busywork to facilitate tens of thousands of new jobs."

"Yes, and the jobs in question largely reflect that," Deborah went along. "There're more than a few humdingers in the bunch, to be sure. Take my own new job as a prime example. 'Temporal dilation assessor."

Horus hardly waited for clarification. "And that is?"

"Basically, I have to gauge whether each hour feels as long as the last, in order to determine whether the flow of time is constant or malleable."

Horus turned disapproving eyes back at Gord. "And what does he do? Watch glass warp?"

"I'm ideating," Gord answered for himself.

Horus met this with silence.

"That's just a fancy word for coming up with ideas, of course."

"I'm sure I know what it means," he remarked. "I just never expected to hear anyone say it."

"Basically, I'm here to do what you do," Gord went on. "Part of it, that is. It's well understood that the balance of any attorney's workday is spent thoughtfully gazing out his window. Except now, you don't have to. That responsibility has passed to me. Think of me as your professional window muse." For the first time, he turned into the car and looked directly at Horus. He was a Human of about 27, with keen eyes and stoic features. "I think you'll be highly satisfied with my work, Mr. Templar. I'm an idea guy from way back."

"Alright," Horus said, folding his arms. "Try me. What were you just thinking about?"

Gord returned to his repose. He let the question hang in the air for a moment. "Drive-thru barbershops."

Horus was equally inclined to let the *answer* hang in the air for a moment. "Come again?"

"Well, imagine it. You pull up, lean your head into the service window, and before you know it, you've got a whole new 'do' without ever leaving the comfort of your own carriage. It'll revolutionize the industry. And it's only the beginning. Just off the top of my head I can imagine a half-dozen other services we could add over time. Mani-pedis; horse grooming. If you can get it within arm's reach of the window, we can work on it."

Horus sighed. "Well, I think I can see where this sudden boom in employment is going."

"But wait – there's more," Deborah said, reaching into a stack of fresh mail and pulling out an envelope with a royal postmark. She waved it at him. "You're not just a beneficiary, Boss. You're going to be a participant."

Without audible protest, Horus took the letter and opened it. "*Painter*?" he read dubiously. "I'm a *painter* now? What kind? Construction? Portraiture?"

"It doesn't say," Deborah said, raising an open palm. "Guess you'll find out when you report to work tomorrow."

Though she played very cool as she continued to gaze off at the other side of the room, Horus could sense her grin, even if he couldn't quite see it. Horus grinned himself. It was all a horrible nuisance, but at least she was having fun at his expense.

After a moment of vacantly picturing the look on Deborah's face, though, Horus managed to remember that Blucille had just joined them, and was currently sitting by the door, completely unengaged. He cleared his throat. "I'm sorry, Ms. Cordon. I'm sure you didn't come here just to listen-in on our trifles."

She shook her head. "I don't mind. Or, well, if I'm bothered at all, it's not your fault. I confess I'm a bit stymied by this whole mass conscription thing myself." She scoffed as she cast a bit of a rueful look at the ground. "I suppose it's just my luck. I'm about the only person I know who didn't get a second job."

Horus had to suppress a chortle, thinking of the hardest-working person he'd ever met bemoaning a lost opportunity to juggle even more work. It was right in line with the way he'd always known her to be. But at the same time, to look at her now, she was nothing like she was before. The old Blucille would've blown in with gale force, commanded their full attention even as she paid them none, promptly stated her business and been gone with hardly time enough for a scathing sarcastic remark or two. Not so, the woman sitting in his office today. She was patient. She was present. She was *peaceful*.

Hardly had Horus had this little epiphany, and Blucille looked back up. "Anyway," she said, "you're right – that's not why I'm here. I came to invite the two of you to a little celebration this evening at the Ecre Point place." She smiled bashfully. "Art and I... we're announcing our engagement."

Deborah gasped, clapping her hands together. "Oh, Blucille, congratulations! We're so happy for both of you!"

"Truly," Horus agreed. "We'd be delighted to attend, Ms. Cordon. In fact, we've been planning on it for some time."

Blucille huffed. "It figures you'd already know. I suppose the big lug gave the whole thing away ahead of time, didn't he?"

"In essence," Horus admitted. "He had to find out when we'd be at leisure to attend a celebration. Oh, he might've tried to pass it off like he had no reason for asking. But you know how Art is."

She laughed. "Yes – the true master of subtlety."

Horus nodded. "Precisely. In the end, the only thing that surprised us at all was when *you* arrived with the official invitation."

"Ah, well... Art had a bit of business come up, or he would've been here. But honestly, I'm happy with the way this played out – being the one to invite you, and all." She hesitated, her eyes shifting distantly. "Really, *everyone* we invited is coming for Art. I... haven't been all that close to anyone besides him in a long time. I wouldn't have been. But out of everyone in Art's inner circle, well... I think I could see being friends with the two of you. Maybe. Someday. If that's alright?"

Horus smiled sarcastically. "I don't know. It sounds like a long shot. But I'd like to believe it's possible."

"My thoughts exactly," Deborah agreed.

"Well, good," she replied, sounding genuinely relieved. "That helps take the pressure off my next request. Can we count on your support at the trial? We had both of you in mind to apply for jury duty. That is, unless you'd like to represent us yourself, Horus?"

"It would be my great pleasure, and honor," Horus replied. "If anything, I'm not sure I ever would've lived it down if the two of you had sought other counsel."

"I wouldn't dream of it," Blucille said, standing back up. "It still pains me to admit, but you're no slouch in court." She turned to Deborah. "And you'll apply for the jury, won't you, Deborah?"

"Of course," Deborah assured her.

Blucille nodded, her gaze falling again. "I think we'll have broad support. But of course, my *family* will be sure to have their say..."

Horus frowned. By now, he knew something of the saga between Blucille and her estranged relatives. "What do you plan to do about that?"

"Art and I are going to face it head-on," she answered quietly. "I'm actually taking him there to meet them tomorrow."

Deborah and Horus exchanged a wide-eyed glance. "The direct approach is probably best," Horus said. "I hope fortune smiles on your courage."

Suddenly, Blucille looked back up. "You know, I'm not even worried. Maybe a bit incensed by the whole idea, but not worried. Whatever's in store, we'll tackle it together. We're ready."

Again – more than at any other point in the conversation – Horus found himself rather amazed. This really was a whole new Blucille Cordon standing in front of him. The sustained, sincere way she looked him in the eye was all the proof he would ever need. "Yes, I believe you are."

They all stood silently for a beat, basking awkwardly in the moment of gratuitous affirmation, before Blucille did something a bit more familiar and cast an anxious look at her pocket watch. "I need to get going," she informed them. "There's still some preparation to be made for the get-together."

"We're prepared to be of help, if it's wanted," Horus offered.

"That's right," Deborah confirmed. "Anything else we might have to do today, I'm sure we can handle it well enough out of Horus' second office."

Horus shook his head at her. "Now, now, Deborah. I certainly have no grounds to consider Ecre Point a 'second office'. We mustn't soon forget: hardly a month ago, it was still Art's most closely-guarded secret."

"I'm beginning to forget already," Deborah replied.

"Well, let's be on our way regardless," Blucille hastened them, opening the door and gesturing out. "You two can argue over custody with Art when he gets there."

"I might just do that," Deborah said. She looked at Horus again, bemused. "You know, he replaced that fishing boat of his, too."

"The one he gave Rythigaar and Imolkyr?" Horus asked. "He said he might. So what if he did?"

She shrugged. "Just thought you might keep that in mind the next time you had to help someone start a new life."

"How fortunate Art is to have a friend who's not afraid to find a use for all his best things."

Both the ladies preceded Horus out the door – which he nearly closed on his own way through – when he suddenly remembered he'd left that strange fellow Gord behind, alone and unattended. He leaned back in. "Gord?" he called, unsure. "Are... are you coming along with us?"

"No, but thank you just the same," Gord replied, throwing a dismissive hand up behind him. "I've got a bit more work to do here. I'll go my own way afterwards. I promise, I'll lock up when I leave."

Horus hesitated. But finally, he could only agree. "Alright."

"One more thing, Mr. Templar," Gord called back, stopping him.

"Yes?"

"You might want to take what your Secretary said to heart – about a second office. At least, for the next few days, or weeks. There're some changes coming to the railway. Changes that might need a bit of time to iron out."

Horus was beside himself, trying to figure out how to respond. He had no idea what Gord was talking about, and no time to ferret out a rational explanation. "Whatever you say, Gord."

"Yes. Do have a good time this evening, Mr. Templar. I'll let you know what I've concluded about the bankruptcy case in the morning."

"Well, thank you." Horus slowly withdrew. "Good night, Gord."

"Good night, Mr. Templar."

Finally, the door creaked until it came shut. The door with the very fine monograms...

...*Horus Templar – Public Defender*

Chapter 3

The rickety old shack was in even worse shape than the last time Art saw it. Siding that should've lasted at least a few more springs had found its way loose, and the piles of glass shards all around the house looked to be stacked much higher than any one set of broken windows could account for. Joining them on the ground was a spattering of rogue shingles – castaways of a sagging, sinking roof. The state of the place was more than unsightly. It was disrepair bordering on capital citation.

Very much against his general preferences, Art commenced to wind himself up for a knock on the front door. But just before he might've knocked, it opened... and standing inside was a tangle of grey scraggles vaguely resembling a man – a man who looked fit for little else than to lead an enormous exodus across both sea and desert sand... or, at the very least, a handful of short people to a solitary old mountain. And judging by the smell – not to mention the flies – it seemed entirely possible he'd already been on both journeys since the last time he bathed.

It was a silent stalemate, there on the threshold. Art was stunned, and surely looked the part. The unidentified mass of unkempt hair, on the other hand, gazed back at him with narrow eyes.

"What're you doin' here, Aaart?" a voice inquired from within the bushy beard area. A voice which – though it *was* a bit froggier than usual – couldn't be mistaken, even if the rest of Steward Jamison had been swallowed up in this massive funk.

"Whatdaya mean, what am I doing here?" Art asked. "You were the one that asked me ta come."

Jamison folded his arms. "I most certainly did nottt."

"Sure ya did. I got your letter. Your exact words were: 'Whatever ya do, don't come over; it's not important'."

The beard-man remained unimpressed. "I know what I wrote. I knew it from the moment I wrote it. Where're we not seeing eye-to-eye here, anyway? I said ***don't*** come. It's ***nottt*** important."

"Well who in the world would write something like that unless it meant I *should* come and it *was* important?"

"Me, for one."

"Okay... okay. Let's try this from the other side-a things. Just what the Heck is so *'not'* important that I *'shouldn't'* come?"

"Whyy, not a thing."

Art pulled at his eyelids. "Well, then, there still has to be something that *is* important, if there's nothing *not* important. Isn't there? Or... doesn't it?"

Jamison slowly blinked his quiet contempt. "What're you trying to saay?"

Art sighed, massaging his head. "I don't even know anymore."

Again, the two of them had reached an impasse.

"Well, seein' as you're here anyway, I suppose ya might as well come in for a spelll," Jamison offered.

Art shrugged. "Whatever."

* * *

Immediately upon entering the living room, Art watched as Jamison plopped down into a groove in his couch that precisely conformed to his body in its frumpiest possible position. Then, with apparently herculean effort, the old man lazily reached out and probed through a bowl of snicky-snacks – one among many strewn all over his filthy coffee table. Only once he'd thoroughly stuffed his face a few times did he seem at all aware of Art's eyes on him. "Kloggem Mills Gooey Globs, Aart? Maybe some Chewapoos?"

"What's going on here, Jamison?" Art asked. "Is this all parta some undercover job you're working right now?"

"W-why no," he replied, barely managing to sit back up. "Aart... I'm retired."

Art reeled. "You're what? But... how? How could you do that?"

"Well, I'm old and broken down enough, aren't I?"

"Oh, yeah... you fit the bill, alright," Art allowed. "More so than I even imagined you could. But what about all that stuff you said before? What about the case never being closed? What about the mole in the SAPD? You and me both know he's still out there! Don't tell me ya gave up on all that just to stuff your face with gummy snacks! I mean, come on, Jamison. I thought you called me over here because you had a new lead or something. A big break in the case!"

"I *didn't* call you over heere. That's exactly the thing I didn't do."

"Don't start that again!" Art replied, pointing for emphasis. "Come on! This is important. Maybe the most important case either one of us has ever been on. And now you're telling me ya just threw in the towel? Just like that?"

Finally, the few visible features of Jamison's face took on a sympathetic cast. He leaned forward and stroked his icky beard a few thoughtful times. Then, he looked back up at Art. "Let me learn ya something, Aart. Something real big they apparently never taught ya in Private Investigator school. When one of us retires, it's never for good. Sure, sure… we let ourselves go for a while. Slip inta deep despondency. We lose sight of everything but the unremitting crumminess of the world. It's at this time that our hardboiled nature reaches its inevitable summit. It's our breaking point, Art. But it's not the end. Something always comes up ta rope us back inta the game. Always. And when it does, we're craftier, shrewder, and more tough-as-nails than ever. That's just how it works."

"Wow," Art marveled, truly taken aback. "I never knew all that."

"Obviously nott." Jamison got up, his cheek bones rising into a warm smile. He came over and set a firm hand on Art's shoulder. "Come on. There's somethin' I want ya ta seee."

After being led to a door behind an inconspicuous pile of old furniture and other garbage, then subsequently down an extremely creepy stairway loaded with cobwebs, Art watched as Jamison footpadded right up to a big, featureless wall in the far back of the musty basement. After a moment of simply looking on, he turned back to Art with his hands on his hips, looking incredibly puffed-out and self-satisfied.

"Yup," Art memorialized the moment, feeling that this was very much the sort of thing he should've expected. "You got a wall, there."

"Not *just* a wall," Jamison boded, reaching down and over to start up a lantern. "I've got something onn it."

Sure enough, as Art squinted and the little lamp leapt to life, he began to see writing – at first, just a few columns of it – and then more noticeably all across the wall. He went in for a closer look, finding that each discreet column had a name at the top, followed by what appeared to be sheer nonsense. He studied one column in particular, at the top of which was the name, 'Cooper Desmondelez'. Directly under it, read: 'eel pond zoo mode'… and then, 'doom creep EZ nod'… and after that, 'demon zed leper co'… and so forth. Hopeless to make heads or tails of the phrases, he did at least feel that the name sounded familiar. And sure enough, as he made a wider survey of the other names, he did recognize one pattern. They were all names of city policemen – or at any rate, as many of them as recognized.

"Well?" Jamison asked. "Whadaya think, huh?"

"I'm not sure what ta think," Art replied, eyes still sweeping over it all. "This looks totally nutzo."

"A true opus usually does." His own roaming look was quite proud. "It's early ta saay, but I think this might be the best work of my whole career."

Art regarded him dubiously. "This has to do with the investigation?"

"W'll acourse it does. What kinda question is thaat?"

"But I thought you were in the dregs of despondency. All that 'dead to the world' stuff you were just saying. How does all this fit in with that?"

He tapped his noggin. "Layers, Aart. It's all about layers. Sure, be despondent. Recognize there's no point and just give up. But under thaat, be more motivated than ya ever imagined you could be."

Tentatively, Art reached out and patted him on the shoulder. "You've got a few too many layers goin' on up there, Buddy."

"I'll be done with it soon, y'know," Jamison said, full of inspirational intonation. "I give it a few more days, tops, and I'll get ya that breakthrough. Come Heck or good golly, I willl."

"Oh-kay," Art replied with great doubt. He could plainly see that whatever was going on here was an enormous exercise in futility. He slowly raised a thumb over his own shoulder. "Well, I got other things ta do. Maybe I oughta just leave ya to your crazy-man wall and get lost. Alright?"

Jamison nodded enthusiastically. "W-sure, sure! I don't mean ta hold ya up all day. Don't forget: I never even meant for you ta come in the first place."

"Right. Sure ya didn't."

"See ya soon, Aart."

Art nodded. "Soon." He turned away. But just before he reached the stairway, Jamison stopped him...

"Heey, wait up a second."

He turned back. "Yes?"

"I just thought ya should know one more thing. When I come outta retirement, I'm gonna do it as an Inspector, not a Detective. I know in my heart I could never go back to detecting. No. No, never. But *inspecting*, now... I...I think I could do thaat."

"Whatever floats your boat, Jamison," Art said, proffering a thumbs-up. At this point, he just wanted to move on to his next order of business...

* * *

"I'm not sure how Art's going to feel about adding all this color in here," Horus boded, even as he strung another line of streamers from wall to wall. "We're certainly impinging on his tribute to monochrome."

"It's a party, Boss. Sacrifices must be made," Deborah replied, setting a small bouquet on the bar. She grinned at him mischievously. "Besides: imagine his relief when he gets to tear all this down."

"You know him so well," Horus doted, securing the end of the long string.

"I can't believe this," Blucille despaired, zooming into the room while holding her hat down. "I can't find the stemmed glasses anywhere!"

"They're over here, Blucille," Deborah assured her, pointing them out from across the bar. "I already set them out."

"Oh, thank goodness," Blucille sighed. She turned to Horus. "What about that ice block I sent you after?"

"Already chipped and in the punch bowl."

"Wow..." she said, after a moment of stunned silence. "I think we're already done." She checked her timepiece. "The guests and the band probably won't even start showing up for another half hour or so. What are we supposed to do until then?"

"Enjoy ourselves, I suppose," Deborah posited with a shrug.

Blucille looked doubtful. "Okay. How do we do that? We haven't exactly 'hung out' before. I'm honestly not sure where to start."

"Well, we're all intelligent people, aren't we?" Deborah encouraged them. "There must be a hundred fun things we can fill the time with."

They all stood around dead silent for a long time, while idea after idea failed to materialize.

"...What was that case you were thinking about taking on?" Blucille asked at length.

"The Hoity Hydroponics bankruptcy suit," Horus answered.

From seemingly nowhere, Deborah produced a file folder. "I brought the papers with me. If we want to look them over a bit more."

Blucille nodded enthusiastically. "Wonderful. Let's do that."

* * *

"So why do you suppose there's no mention of President Cortland on the preliminary list of witnesses?" Deborah asked, still leaning over Art's bar.

"You don't mean Ambrosia Cortland?" Blucille inquired in return, while she lounged in a chaise, staring down at another set of documents while her legs absently kicked behind her. "As in, the very same president of the Adopt a Sponsor Foundation? If I had to guess, she's probably too mired in that suit right now to appear at a second one."

"She's right, of course," Horus said from his own seat at the piano bench, holding another sheet in front of his nose. "It says here that her testimony will be admitted by... *oh*, here we go..." he lamented, having stupidly wandered right into a most unwelcome gridlock. "...Adififit? Ad...adiv...afiditiv...?"

"*Dianodes*," Blucille marveled. "Horus – you can't say 'affidavit'?"

Horus was temporarily too embarrassed to speak. Finally, he forced a grin and shrugged. "Well, doesn't everybody have a word like that?"

"For me, it's 'peripheral'," Deborah covered for him. "Trips me up every time."

"But you just said it right..." Blucille pointed out, still obviously, deviously pleased.

"Chock it up to a first time for everything," Deborah dismissed it.

Blucille turned back to Horus, appearing quite ready for some serious joshing at his expense. Mercifully, however, she was cut off...

"Hey, compadres," Art called out from the doorway. "What's shakin'?"

"Art," Blucille called back warmly, getting up and crossing the room to greet him with an embrace.

"There's my Pumpernickel Petunia," Art doted, taking her in his arms.

"I'm so glad Detective Jamison didn't hold you up long," she said, pulling back as she searched him. "What did he want to talk to you about, anyway?"

Art shrugged. "Nothing."

Blucille scoffed. "Sure he didn't. Come on, Art – you're no good at this. What did he lure you out there to say?"

"Nothing," Art insisted, seeming a bit wounded. "Honestly."

"Yeah... 'nothing'." She grinned, shaking her head at him. "That's what everyone says when they're hiding something."

"That's also what everyone says when they're *not* hiding something," Art riposted. "Look: I already had ta argue about this with him the first time. He offered me some disgusting snacks and showed me a wall he scribbled all over and that was it. Can't we just be happy I'm here?"

"I'm sorry. You know it just makes me nervous – the two of you conspiring. The High Constable made it very clear he wanted the mole case sealed off. Not to mention how unhappy the mole himself would be, if he knew you were still gunning for him."

"Not ta worry, Sugar Snap. Jamison's been playing it low-key... and I mean about as low-key as you can get. And we're both agreed: We won't make a move until we have the smoking gun."

Blucille sighed. "Forget I mentioned it. Your assurances only make me feel worse." She set a hand on his upper arm. "You're right. You're here now. That means it's party time."

"Now you're talkin'," he went along, giving her a squeeze around the shoulder. He turned his attention to the room at large, seeming to take it all in for the first time. "Some decorating job you guys did, huh?"

"Oh?" Blucille intoned. "You really like what we put up?"

"Uh-huh," he said with a nod. "I'll like it even better when I get to take it down."

"Impeccable timing," Horus thought aloud, his gaze trained on the doorway. "It looks like the other guests have started to arrive already."

Art smiled warmly as he led Blucille, Horus and Deborah to welcome the newcomers. "Elmer!" he called out. "I'm so glad you could make it!"

"Elmer?" Horus interjected. "Could this be Elmer Ehmstein, Private Investigator extraordinaire?"

"Eh," Elmer confirmed.

"And look!" Art exclaimed. "You even brought your lovely wife, Ermine Ermstrong!"

"Hi, Art; so good to see you!" Ermine said.

Elmer and Ermine proceeded down the line, receiving handshakes and words of welcome even as a queue began to form behind them.

"Say, I'll bet you guys have never met ol' Franko Steratore," Art said as the next guest stepped forward. He was an aging Human who made no pretense against presenting himself with bad posture and a long face. "Howya doin', Sport?"

"Please stop calling me that," Franko replied, turning cheerless eyes up at Art, Blucille, Horus, and Deborah in turn.

"Ha! Same Franko as always!" Art chuckled. "Don't let his razor-sharp sarcasm fool ya," he explained to the rest of the welcome wagon. "This guy's as good-natured as they come. You'll never guess in a million years how we met."

Unable to pick up on even the slightest glimmer of any kindred spirit between them, Horus was at a loss – at least as much as both the ladyfolk, who certainly appeared disinclined to venture any kind of guess. For his part, he was in no hurry to speculate, either.

"You're probably right," Blucille finally put in. "How *did* you meet?"

"It was this money laundering case I was working, years and years ago. There were lots of eyes on the company books – including Franko's. I could bore ya with all kinds of details, but the real kicker is, I was sure *he* was the one that did it! And thanks ta all my hard work, I nearly had everyone else convinced of it, too." He made an incredibly small pinching gesture in the air. "I tell ya: I had him *this close* to the chopping block! I mean, he was a goner for sure! Fortunately, of course, he was absolved at the last minute. A bunch of evidence I completely missed came out and they caught the real perp. Wouldn't ya know? Turns out it was some of the sloppiest work I ever did!" He laughed. "Anyway, I made a point of apologizing for the whole misunderstanding. I'll never forget Franko's words, that day. Do ya remember what ya said, Franko?"

Franko shrugged. "Guess it was something like, 'Don't worry about it'."

"That was it exactly!" Art elated. "We've been thick as thieves ever since." He slapped Franko a good one on the back as he buddied right up to him.

Again, there was a bit of awkward tension before Blucille rallied the words to get things rolling. "Thank you for coming out to support Art and me, Mr. Steratore."

"Gosh only knows why I bother," Franko replied. He turned back to Art. "I don't suppose you've got anything fit for a Human to eat around here?"

Art could only look questioningly at the three who had actually put the party together.

"Uh, well, we did put out a few loaves of sliced bread," Deborah offered.

"Ah, sliced bread – the biggest thing since itself," Franko commented, sans any real enthusiasm. "At least it'll be easy on my ulcers."

With that, he walked away, to the immediate relief of everyone besides Art. Horus, however, did not enjoy a long reprieve from his discomfort. He turned back towards the doorway, jumping ever so slightly at the sight of the next guest...

"Hello, Counselor," Dr. Nokkaeru said, staring right back up at him with her icy goggles.

"Hello, Doctor," he replied, taking a moment just to rationalize her sudden appearance.

"You seem surprised to see me. I wonder why that should be."

Horus scratched thoughtfully behind his ear. "I suppose there's just something about your ongoing friendship with Art that I haven't wrapped my head around yet."

"Such comradery often develops between two people of exceptional brilliance. I wouldn't expect you to understand."

Horus grinned a bit of a mean-spirited grin. "Speaking of the exceptionally brilliant with whom you have close association, where is Forasius? I'm sure Art and Blucille were quite clear that everyone should bring their plus one."

Nokkaeru brooded silently for a beat or two. "Mercifully, he was unable to attend."

"You didn't even tell him about this, did you?" Horus ventured.

"Thus, where the mercy comes in. It was certainly more merciful for me to omit any mention of this gathering than to suture him to the carpet to prevent his coming." She trained a passing glance in Deborah's direction, who was providentially engaged in welcoming other guests. "But as for you, Counselor, I am unsurprised to find your own 'plus one' in attendance."

Horus kept up an impassive front. "Trying those old tricks again, are we? What's the matter, Doctor? Does the mention of your husband really offend you that much? Or, is this just your way of getting my attention?"

Nokkaeru shook her head. "I was merely trading one jab for another. I have no need of such mundane antics to secure your attention. And as for the matter of Forasius, we will discuss it more seriously tomorrow – bright and early. Until then, you have my permission to enjoy your evening."

She strutted away, leaving Horus greatly perplexed, and more than vaguely troubled. He was sure he had no plans of seeing Nokkaeru tomorrow. He puzzled with a frown as he watched her go right up to Art, who greeted her with a smile and a wave...

"Hey, Doc," he said. "How's it goin'?"

"I am well-pleased to be in your most amicable company, Friend Mallard," she answered. "Let the record show that I believe you are making a grievous blunder by pursuing nuptials. Even so, may your impending marriage be more propitious than the norm."

"Far out and groovy," Art replied with a laugh, coolly covering for the fact that he obviously had no idea what she was talking about. They passed each other by, with Art on his way to rejoin Horus. He patted Horus' shoulder as he turned to stand beside him, facing back into the room. "Horus..." he said.

Horus nodded at him. "Art..."

"I'm really glad you're here, Buddy," Art explained. "I didn't want ya ta feel left out of the greeting just 'cause you wound up a part of the welcoming committee yourself. You and Debs are easily in my top ten-or-so honored guests. I hope ya know that."

"I *am* honored, Art," Horus assured him, putting a hand on Art's far shoulder. "Not just to be here, but to play such a crucial role in the trial to come."

"You're going to represent us? You don't have to, ya know. I've got Eb on the back burner if you'd rather just put in for jury duty or something."

"No, I'm only too happy to." Horus chuckled. "Though I wonder if I'm doing you any favors. You'd probably be even better off with Eb."

"Probably," Art joshed him. "You'll do fine, Horus. I have no doubt." He looked across the way and caught Blucille's eye as he reflected dreamily on it all. "It's still hard ta believe this is really happening."

"There were many who thought it unlikely from the start," Horus admitted.

"Don't I know it."

Horus looked at him. "How did you manage it, Art? The proposal, I mean. It occurs to me, just now: if I ever had to pop the question, I wouldn't have the first clue how to do it. What was your method?"

"You're looking for a pointer or two from the baron of hearts, Horus?" Art asked roguishly.

Horus shrugged. "Well, why not?"

Art stepped back and framed the scene. "Okay. It went like this. I took her hand, see. Then, I looked her straight in the eye. And I said: 'Hey, Blucille: can I please get married to ya?"

Horus didn't blink. "And, that worked?"

"Well *yeah*," Art intoned. "I mean obviously. Here we are."

Horus pursed his jowls. "In that case, I suppose fortune truly is on your side, my friend."

Just then, there was a stumbling noise in the stairway. Art and Horus whirled around, finding a Human already struggling to aright himself after crashing to his knees at the foot of the stairs. They instinctively rushed to pick him up – one under each arm.

"Easy, there," Horus coached the man, taking his first real look at him. He didn't appear to be anyone he'd ever met before. He had skinny – almost gaunt – features, and his eye on the side nearest to Horus was covered by a massive adhesive bandage.

"Sorry – so clumsy..." the man breathed. "I thought I was in the clear once I made it to the stairs."

"Yeah, sorry 'bout the mess up there," Art said. "I tried ta beat down a good path, but..." He stopped up. "Hey, who *are* you, anyway?"

Horus' brow furrowed. "This isn't one of your guests?"

Art shook his head. "I've never seen this guy before."

"I'm so sorry," the man apologized again. "I see you have a get-together going on here. I don't mean to intrude. But... well, it's rather urgent."

"What do you need?" Horus asked.

"I... I could use some legal counsel, I think," he answered. "I might be in a lot of trouble. Is there an attorney named Horus Templar here? I was told he would be."

Horus and Art exchanged a glance. "*My* name is Horus Templar," Horus said. "How can I help you?"

* * *

"So there I was, just stepping out from between two buildings, when all of a sudden this maniac came dashing by and threw me out of the way," the man recounted. "I hit my eye on a hanging sign and collapsed to the ground, bleeding. Next thing I knew, there was a policeman standing over me. I realized he must've been chasing the maniac, and I pointed the way he went."

Horus looked on intensely. He, Art, Deborah, and Blucille had taken the man to a back room to let him have his say. "What then?"

The man's arms flapped against his sides. "Then nothing, I guess. I started fading in and out. I got a pretty good concussion. Some of the details are still hazy." He thought on it for a spell. "I...I think there might've been a second cop at one point. But I don't remember where he went."

"They must've taken you to the station," Blucille put in. "Taken your statement?"

The man nodded. "I told them everything I told you. But I... I asked them who they were after – who it was that ran into me." His voice waxed grave, almost haunted. "They said it was *him*. They said it was Left-Foot Lazarus."

"What did you have to offer to prove that you weren't Lazarus yourself?" Blucille demanded.

"Come now, Ms. Cordon. This isn't an interrogation," Horus talked her down.

"No, it's a fair question," the man insisted. "I... I didn't have *anything* to say for myself, really. But the officer on the scene – he ruled me out on the grounds that my feet were too big. The shoe print left behind was very small – almost child-sized. But I wear size 13."

Blucille huffed. "Anyone can stuff his shoes. You say you *wear* size 13. Let's see if the shoe fits."

Horus shot her an icy glance. "If you're going to be this combative, perhaps you ought to return to the party. Do you honestly think the rest of the SAPD didn't have the presence of mind to check for that themselves?"

"I think Pooky's being reasonable," Art interjected. "Wouldn't it better to know for yourself than assume?"

Horus turned to Deborah, who didn't speak... but her expression was enough to divert any appeal he might make to her. He could see it in her eyes: she thought they were right. He was taken aback...

"You... want to see my foot?" the man asked.

Horus sighed. "That would seem to be the majority opinion."

He set his jaw, before finally looking down. "Alright." He reached for and unlaced his left shoe. He slipped out of it, then removed his sock as well. He held the great big foot up for all to see, wiggling his toes for emphasis. "There you are."

Horus nodded. "Thank you. That certainly satisfies me."

"I appreciate that," the man said, tugging his sock back on. "I only wish I felt like it was enough to satisfy the police, too."

"Why wouldn't it be?" Horus asked, leaning back in his chair. "If your foot was too big for the crime, it would seem to me that you're already ruled out."

He shook his head. "I've got a nagging feeling it's not going to be that simple. The fact of the matter is, Mr. Templar, I'm the only person of interest in about the biggest case this city's seen. The *only* person. When you add that up with the way they found me – how motivated they are to close this case..." He looked nervously over at Blucille before averting his eyes. "I hate to even say it out loud, but... what if they find a way to pin it on me? What if they... well... dress up the facts a bit?"

"Dress up the facts?" Blucille repeated, folding her arms. "You mean lie and cheat? Falsify evidence? Persecute an innocent man while the real psycho gets to run amuck another day? Listen here, you..."

"*Blucille,*" Horus cautioned her. "I appreciate your motivation to uphold the SAPD's good name. I share it. But you know as well as I do that the

Czarina's going to be after her pound of flesh. Left Foot Lazarus has been a thorn in her side for months now. She'll jump at the first chance she gets to prove her iron fist always prevails."

Blucille frowned, but it was enough to silence her.

Horus returned his attention to the man. "What's your name, Sir?"

"Adam," he replied. "Adam Oppenheimer."

"Adam..." Horus mused. "An unusual name."

"I'm a bit of an unusual man," Adam admitted. "I always seem to be stumbling into things. But this little pratfall... this tops them all." His one exposed eye searched pleadingly. "Do you think you can help me, Mr. Templar? Are you willing to?"

Horus made a quick study of the room. Blucille was disgusted. Art's features were drawn back comically; he shook his head with clenched teeth. And Deborah – Deborah remained unconvinced as well. Why? He couldn't reckon. Here was a man in obvious need of help. But apparently, Horus was the only one who could see that. Much as he respected the wisdom of his friends, their reticence ultimately made what he had to do that much clearer to him...

"Yes," Horus answered. He reached out and shook Adam's hand. "I'll do what I can for you, Mr. Oppenheimer."

Chapter 4

A pre-dawn trip to the employment bureau sufficed to clarify Horus' inconvenient new calling – he would be painting interior walls from 6:00 to 10:00 three days a week and 19:00 to 1:00 another three nights a week. His first assignment: 8788 Vitriol Parkway in the foreign dignitary annex. For the first time in as long as he could remember, he found himself in public sans suit and tie, having been quickly fitted with layers of denim and huge, baggy overalls, leaving him feeling simultaneously under and over-dressed. Paint roller on pole extender slung over his shoulder and a big can of some drab color or other in his off hand, Horus marched out to meet what nevertheless promised to be a bright and cheerful day.

...Well, bright, anyway.

After all, he could only go so far before all the little warning bells started to stack up. First, it wasn't lost on him that he was headed for a borough of expatriates. Arriving at the mouth of Vitriol Parkway only reinforced his misgivings, where he quickly noted the round domiciles, the low mailboxes, and persuasion of the few residents who happened to be out and about on their lawns. But of course, all hope was finally lost when he arrived at the cul-de-sac, finding her goggles trained on him from the deep shadows of the front door at 8788.

"Good morning, Counselor," Nokkaeru chimed, inasmuch as she would ever chime anything. "How pleasant to see that dumbfounded expression I left you with last night replaced by grim understanding."

"Good morning, Doctor," Horus replied, out-and-out grumbling – avoiding direct eye contact as he strode up. "Your captive audience, reporting as ordered." He walked right past her, straight into the house.

"Now wait just a moment," she scoffed, following him in. "Aren't you the least bit curious how I managed to arrange for this?"

"Not really," he answered, surveying the main room. "I'm sure it was incredibly clever. Congratulations. Now whatever you have to say, let's get it over with."

"Oh... I seem to have inspired a particularly bad humor in you," Nokkaeru intoned, sounding most pleased. "This may very well work to my advantage." She continued past him towards a back door. "Hold on. There are other parties who might help illustrate my dilemma." She opened the door and leaned out. "*Forasius*! Come in here this instant."

On command, Forasius soon appeared. "Yes, Love?"

"I have a guest. You will remember Horus Templar, I trust."

"Ah, yes!" Forasius exclaimed. "Welcome to my dear Nokkaeru's local residence, Mr. Templar! Tell me: To what do we owe the pleasure of your visit?"

Horus would've been much assuaged by the mere appearing of Dr. Forasius, and all his exuberant charisma – in every way, the perfect foil for his wife – if it weren't for the fact that his question caught him flat-footed. "Well... our dear Doctor alluded to some sort of conversation she meant to have with me this morning." A conversation she suggested was to be about the very man she'd just summoned, for that matter – a curiosity he decided to omit. "It was my understanding that I would be starting a new profession as a Painter at this time, but it would seem she somehow managed to lure me out here on a false pretense."

"There is nothing 'false' about my pretenses, Counselor," Nokkaeru challenged. "Your appointment as Painter is quite legitimate, and binding. I suggest you commence your work immediately."

Horus frowned at the grey walls, then down at his can of grey paint. With a faint sigh, he hunkered down and quickly managed to pry the lid off with his sturdy claws.

"Ah! May I assume you chose the color yourself, Dear?" Forasius asked, once the paint was open for all to see.

"I did," Nokkaeru deigned to answer.

"A most appealing choice," he said. "Ever so slightly bluer than the present decorum."

"Yes. So I intended."

"I have always favored blue," Forasius mused.

"I as well."

"So invigorating. Magisterial as the sky and sea."

"Pallid. Cold, and lifeless."

Not knowing any better, Horus simply dunked the roller in the bucket and busied himself rolling thick swathes on the wall, hoping his quick action and their meandering discussion would be sufficient to distract from the way he failed to keep a few small dribbles of paint from accenting the floor as well.

"...Anyway, we digress," Nokkaeru announced. "Forasius: You will recall the ridiculous ultimatum you put forward the other day. Recount it to Mr. Templar now."

Horus paused his rolling and looked back over his shoulder. Though of course, Forasius' features were veiled under his Plague Doctor garb, both their glances managed to be about equally uncertain.

"I... believe I said..." Forasius cleared his throat, reaching out with one talon in true soliloquy fashion. "'My dear, my love – the joy of my existence'..."

"Oh, do cut your blubbering short and come to the point," Nokkaeru interjected.

"Ah. A summary, then. Of course, I reminded you that my internship here would be coming to a close shortly."

Both of them hesitated.

"And?" Nokkaeru urged him at length.

"I... elucidated that when it does, I will be returning to our homeland. And I asked that you return with me."

Horus' ears pinned back as the gravity of this little rehearsal really began to weigh on him. He looked at each of them in turn, feeling ill at ease to be clued-in on this extremely personal conversation.

"That is correct," Nokkaeru finally summed it up. "You are no longer needed here, Forasius. Remove yourself at once."

Forasius took only a moment to nod. "Of course, my dear." He turned to go and started off.

At this point, Horus had already had too close a look at their toxic relationship. He hated to see someone as good-natured as Forasius endure endless disrespect. "Forasius, wait," he called out. "Why do you let her cast you off like that? Order you around brusquely all the time?"

There was a warm glint in Forasius' goggles. "Why, Mr. Templar – that is like asking why a fellow would stop to feel a summer breeze in his feathers. Her fiery aspect brings back more fond memories than I can number. It is just as she ever was, any time she would assume the lead in our surgical operations." He turned his dreamy look at Nokkaeru herself. "My dear, do you remember that Mesomela chap who got his stomach twisted, and it fell to us to operate? You had hardly begun your practice on exotic specimens then. Does our own Horus Templar resemble him rather remarkably?"

"*Go,*" she said.

He nodded again. "Right. Adieu, my love! And farewell, Mr. Templar!"

The door promptly shut.

"Now you see the most regrettable predicament in which I find myself," Nokkaeru premised. "The predicament of having to make a *choice*. Either to hold this course or reverse another choice I labored to buy myself many years ago."

"I see you're in the midst of some... *drama*, yes. But why involve me?" Horus asked. "If this is any kind of quandary, why not ask your *friend*, instead? Why not ask Art?"

She shook her head. "Much as I respect his formidable reserves of genius, Art Mallard has lately revealed his one fatal flaw. He is a romantic. A friend's advice will not serve well where his judgment would tend to be compromised. But as for you, Counselor – is it not your duty to offer *counsel*? Your first and truest duty, for which you are far better suited than these splotches on my wall bode that you shall ever be in your latest profession? Then counsel me now."

Horus pursed his jowls, briefly scratching under his chin. "I think you should go back with him."

"*Augh*!" she protested, ruffling prickly feathers as she turned away. "That is *not* what you were supposed to advise!"

He shrugged, unable to stop himself from grinning. "Sorry. But what can I say? It seems the sensible choice to me."

"Sensible? I think not. More like *sentimental*. I depended on you to be the voice of unfeeling pragmatism in this," she despaired. "You who so adroitly rationalize your fainthearted avoidance of all close attachment."

Horus frowned at her assessment of his character. Suddenly, though, he recognized an opportunity to nudge a nearby space rug over his paint spills while her back was turned, which he quickly and stealthily seized on with his foot.

"...You have no idea what it's like to be wed to someone who is always so... so blasted light. And *cheerful*."

"Sounds like torture," Horus sympathized, only to drizzle yet more paint as he tried to return to work.

"Entirely the wrong sort of torture, regrettably," she lamented. "Horus: the world he lives in is quite different from reality. In his world, joy has more merit than grief. Agreeable turns of fate aren't simply the misrepresentative whim of disaster – to strategically stall its own advance until a more opportune moment should arise. His is a chronic lunacy, and I fear the effects of long-term exposure. My countless attempts to cure him have all failed. I... had thought that leaving him behind might teach him some wisdom. But no. When inevitably he found a way to follow me here, I could see from the first: he's the same as I left him. A hopeless, insufferable nincompoop."

"You left him?" Horus asked, turning a bit too fast. At this point, his inability to control the basic trajectory of the paint from his brush was not only visible, but audible. Nokkaeru looked back, turning her cold glance first at the newest, greatest splatter on her floor, then up at him. He grinned nervously. "I can fix that."

"You can, and you will," she said in a low voice – nodding, and craning her head dejectedly. "This was a grave miscalculation on my part. I went to such lengths to hear you affirm that I must stay on here, as the one valid medical professional in all of St. Argonsburg – an assurance that should have taken mere moments to secure. But instead, you chose *his* side. And now, I shall have to endure your presence for weeks, while you cluelessly renovate my home."

"If I may ask..." Horus put in, working outward rather aimlessly from the first few streaks on the wall. "Since you evidently had the answer you wanted already firmly in mind ahead of time, why seek anyone's input at all? Could it be that deep down, you have mixed feelings, Doctor?"

"Oh, yes – a most volatile mixture," she admitted. "Frustration, fury, annoyance. Exhaustion. *Exasperation...*"

"I mean besides those."

She scoffed. "What other 'feeling' would you suggest, Counselor?"

"What about love? Do you love him, Doctor? Did you ever?"

She declined to answer, at first. Finally, she meandered toward the back door. When she was only a few feet from the threshold, she spoke in a low voice. "Even if I ever did, it only brings what I must do now more clearly into focus."

Horus made no effort to understand. "What do you mean?"

She set a talon on the door, cracking it open as she looked back at him, her fateful aspect reflecting in the eyes of her mask. "Horus Templar, I see it is high time that I elucidate one of life's greatest truths. If you don't choose misery for yourself, it will inevitably be chosen for you." She slowly leaned her head outside. "Forasius! Undoubtedly you are still skulking about out there. I command you to return."

Promptly, he appeared. "At your beck and call, my love. How can I be of service?"

"Forasius: Counselor Templar and I have discussed your proposition, and we have reached the following conclusion: I shall not be returning with you. I will remain behind."

"*What*? No," Horus protested reflexively. They both regarded him. "That is, well... that's not what I advised her to do at all!"

"In fairness, that is true," Nokkaeru admitted. "Yet it was the content of your counsel that made me sure. For that, I thank you." She crossed the room. "And now, I must be off. Good day to you, Mr. Templar. Please do exercise more care in your work from now on."

Just like that, she was gone.

Horus was overcome with sympathy, seeing Forasius stare blankly at the closed door. "I'm so sorry, Doctor," he said finally. "I really did my best to change her mind, but I'm afraid it was quite useless. She has... a very contrary way about her."

"I have noticed that," he replied, his voice nearly a sigh. At length, he turned to Horus. "It's quite alright, Mr. Templar. I don't doubt you were a stalwart advocate. You have my sincere thanks. But I suspect she had already resolved to do this in any event."

"Well, for what it's worth, I share your disappointment. It would've been a great comfort to see her return home."

Forasius' head craned down thoughtfully on the end of his long neck. "I *am* disappointed, if not surprised. Nevertheless, I emerge from this endeavor with much to be thankful for. These last few weeks have been a dream. I will cherish the memory. And I will keep my hope alive that, perhaps, she may yet come back, one day."

Horus waxed thoughtful as well. "If I might presume to advise you legally, perhaps there's something more you could do than merely hope."

Forasius gave him a canted look. "Such as?"

Horus shrugged. "I'm not well versed in the laws of Roemnar, but is it at all far-fetched to petition for a more permanent reassignment? One that would put the two of you back into proximity? You're a medical professional of some distinction, I'm sure – and you're the one living stateside, where you can better leverage your influence. Isn't it possible you could get her transferred back? If nothing else, the two of you are married, and that *is* a legal status. You might have more leverage than you think."

Forasius only nodded absently. "We *are* married. We're constrained to that both now, and forever more. But love, fondness, closeness – can I demand such things from her? I would not if I could. We choose very little for ourselves in this life, Mr. Templar, but the little that we do is the more precious for it. Her marriage to me, of course, was not within her power to choose, but how she engages with it certainly is. Above all, love must be sincere. If it is her wish to be apart from me, I will respect it. My own love for her leaves me no alternative."

Involuntarily, Horus grinned. "She's a fool to turn you down, Forasius. You love her much better than I would've thought possible."

"A quizzical opinion, Counselor," Forasius replied as he ambled over towards the wall, seeming to have recovered his cheerfulness. "Although, I admit: There are times I begin to suspect her charming disposition is less than universally appealing. One of life's little mysteries, I suppose. But now, what is to become of you, Mr. Templar? Are you the equal to this painting job? Or do I rightly guess that you feel somewhat out of your depth?"

Horus looked at the stupid, amorphous mess he'd made so far and sighed. "This isn't my area of expertise."

"Nor mine. But I have a steady talon, and a few hours before it must be used in surgical endeavors. And after all, we have some wits about us, don't we? Perhaps between the two of us, we can contrive an effective method."

Horus nodded his gratitude. "Much obliged. I'll take any help I can get."

* * *

Meanwhile, on the far side of suburbia, Art put his nose in a tall stack of papers as they were ambling along in the idyllic heat of day. By now, he and Blucille were well on their way to keep a fateful appointment with her estranged parents. Engaging with a bit of light reading, Art could have been the very picture of calm, cool assurance. Blucille, on the other hand, was personifying other emotions...

"I just know they're going to make me regret sending that letter," she said quickly, her heels tapping hard on the sidewalk. "We should've pressed our advantage and dropped in on them unannounced. Letting them know we were coming ahead of time was a major strategic blunder. It means they'll be *prepared*."

"Yeah, maybe," Art assured her, having long ago tuned out.

"Honestly, there's no telling what we'll be walking into, Art. The potential guest list alone could derail everything a hundred different ways."

He flipped a page. "Sure it could."

"Just off the top of my head I could see them inviting Aunt Omarosa. She wasn't on the first jury, so I'm sure they spun the story of the trial their own way. Her guilt trips are the stuff of legend."

"Neat."

"Then there's Uncle Imhotep, who never fails to make everything about *him*. I mean, even if I'd cut them all off for the last *twenty years*, I'm sure he'd..." She came to an abrupt halt as she looked up, her eyes searching frantically in all directions. "Art, where'd you go?"

"Oh, sorry," he said, once again conspicuous the moment he put down his paperwork. "Guess I really got pulled into the story there for a bit."

"Another manuscript?" she asked.

"Yup."

She started them walking again at the same clip as before. "Alright... tell me about it. I could use the distraction. What's the title?"

He flipped back to the front. "*The Nephew's Uncle*."

She made a face. "What in the world is it about? Besides the obvious?"

"I dunno," he said, trying to find where he left off. "I'm not very far in yet. Don't really remember much about the author's brief, either. Said something about it being a prequel to this other story about a sorceress and a mystical sock drawer. A big cat, too – I don't remember what kind. A puma or a jaguar, probably."

"Okay..." she said, hardly pretending to understand. "But now, if they invite Cousin Argyle..."

"Blucille," Art interjected. "Come on, now. Don't sweat it. You said you weren't even worried about this."

"I know... and I wasn't," she groaned, pulling her hat down tight over her head.

"Then don't be now. Just relax, Ginger Snap. We got this in the bag."

"Right. Of course, you're right."

He ruffled his papers rigid. "Here, I'll read ya a bit. 'This is a story from way back, when your grandson was a gnarled old geezer'."

"Oh no! There it is!" she cried, stopping and pointing. "I see their house!"

"Well, yeah; that's where we've been going," Art chuckled. "What'd ya expect to see in its place?"

"A big smoking crater wouldn't have been so bad," she mumbled.

"Hey, now. You don't really mean that. This is your family, Blucille."

"Oh, I know. I don't think I could ever hate them completely. But that's part of what makes me so blasted furious with them, you know?"

“Not really,” Art admitted with a shrug. ”But come on. The moment ya see your folks face-to-face, it’s gonna make everything that much easier. It can’t be as bad as you’re thinking.”

She stared blankly down the road. “I suppose you’re right. Nothing can be *that* bad.”

“Well, then… here we go,” he coached her. And as he offered his arm, they continued again.

About the time they were a few feet from the front stoop – an approach that seemed to slow, the closer they got – the vague rumor of some berserk army of small children engulfed them before they even realized they’d been flanked. A rolling wave of little black-furred arms, ears, and snouts burst around them and crowded the doorway – all an inscrutable mess of pushing, shoving, and shouting. Art turned his shell-shocked eyes at an even more shell-shocked Blucille. But just as she returned his gaze, her agape mouth suddenly curled up into a mischievous grin.

“You know these kids?” Art inquired over the bustle.

“No,” she answered slyly. “Not a one of them.”

Art studied her. “Why’re you so happy about it?”

“Maybe this means they moved.”

“Blucille?!” They heard behind them. “Is that really you?”

They turned around, and there they found a young Mesomela woman who much resembled Blucille – on the rare occasions she wasn’t wearing a great wide hat, anyway. The only other apparent difference was the way her eyelids looked like they’d been open since the onset of the Static Era.

“Redna…” Blucille gasped.

“Blucille… it really is you,” Redna replied, while they both stared at each other in amazement. The silence between them was loud. But not quite as loud as the herd of youngsters.

At length, Blucille raised a hand, pointing back down at all the tiny hooligans. “These are yours, I take it?”

Redna nodded. “Yeah.”

Blucille’s eyes danced over them for a moment. When she began to appear dizzy, she looked back up. “How many?”

Redna sighed viscerally. “I have no idea.”

For a while, the chaos raged on, until Blucille abruptly rallied her wits. “I’m sorry; where are my manners? Art, this is Redna, my sister. Redna, this is Art Mallard… my fiancé.”

This announcement sufficed to renew Redna's conspicuous disbelief. "Your what?"

"You heard right," Blucille assured her. "He's my fiancé."

"And pleased ta meet ya," Art said, offering a handshake.

Redna woodenly accepted his hand, looking at Blucille. "Do Mom and Dad know about this?"

"Well... well, yes," Blucille answered, perplexed. "You aren't here to see me, then? That is... I mean... they didn't invite you over for the occasion?"

"No, I'm afraid not," Redna answered. "I bring the kids over a lot. Guess it was just good timing."

This also perplexed Blucille. "You bring your children to these people?"

"Oh yeah."

She frowned. "But why?"

Suddenly, the front door opened. Instantly, the kids were all standing in a perfect row at silent attention.

"That's why," Redna quietly explained.

"Well, look who it is," a stately Mesomela woman said as she emerged from the shadow of the threshold, followed by a Mesomela man with a grey, grim muzzle sporting oversize, squarish spectacles. "Dear, you'll remember our daughter, Blucille?"

"Of course," her husband answered. "What a surprise to see she remembers *us*."

For all his earlier confidence, Art was certainly more cowed by the thick front of passive-aggression than he expected. Blucille was also momentarily dumbstruck. Her mother looked right past them, smiling slightly more sincerely as she did...

"Ah, Redna... you're here, too. How perfect. Why don't the two of you come in for a while with the children?"

"Wait," Blucille insisted. Her ears pinned back as her folks turned their gazes back on her. "I... brought someone with me." She gestured to her side. "*Mother... Father,*" she said, each word a special pain. "This is Artimus Mallard."

Art cleared his throat. "Uh, yeah, that's me," he went along, in a somewhat overly manly voice. He waved. "Hiya."

"Oh, yes. Your... 'gentleman caller'," Blucille's mother intoned, her eyes protesting his very existence.

"Art, these are my *parents*," Blucille formally introduced them, her teeth nearly getting in the way. "Ednice Drusilla and Pileser Shealtiel."

Art reached out to shake Ednice's hand first. "Pleased ta meet ya, er... may I call you Ednice?"

She shook his hand with a wide, toothy smile. "You may not."

"Mrs. Drusilla?"

The shaking and smiling continued. "No."

Art was at a loss. "Surely not 'Future Mom'?"

"*Especially* not that."

Finally, the shake ended. Art rubbed the back of his neck. "Well, then... what should I call ya?"

"Why, nothing at all, Dear."

He chuckled, trying not to swallow his molten tongue. "Okay." He moved down the line to Blucille's father. "Pleased ta meet you too, Sir."

"I can't imagine why," Pileser replied, keeping his arms folded.

Art tugged at his collar. He angled a squiggly smile at Blucille, who was no help. He had no choice but to return to the iron wall of her parents and force himself to say... something. Anything at all...

"So, uh... did Blucille happen ta mention that she and I are gettin' hitched?"

"Why don't we discuss that over lunch?" Ednice offered – an idea that, while delivered with plenteous condescending overtures, seemed impossibly gracious next to everything else so far. "I brought a hypsilophodont up from the meat cellar this morning. We were just about to carve out the heart."

"That *is* your specialty," Blucille mumbled.

Ednice swung the door wide, clearly choosing not to hear her daughter. "Do come in."

* * *

"So. What is it you do for a living, Mr. Mallard?" Ednice asked, setting her silverware down and folding her hands in a show of feigned interest.

Art – who'd naturally just taken a bite – choked down what he had in his mouth as fast as he could. "Well, I cut my teeth as a Private Investigator," he said.

"A *Private Investigator*? How quaint," Ednice replied airily.

"We've even worked a few cases together," Blucille pointed out rather meekly before wiping her mouth.

"Yeah! That's right!" Art jumped enthusiastically on her point. "And one of 'em was a doozy." He even dared rub his curled-up fingers confidently against his blazer. "I, uh... don't suppose ya heard about the big breakup of the Digit Cults?"

"No," Pileser answered with a frown.

Art deflated. "Well... I mean... it was a pretty big one."

"Hm," Pileser said dubiously, picking up a newspaper.

"Alright, so that's *one* career," Ednice rejoined. She turned to Blucille. "And you, Dear... you're some sort of legal secretary in Hamilton Blackforest's office now, aren't you?"

"I'm his premier Assistant District Attorney!" she fairly barked. By all appearances, she surprised herself more than anyone. But her jowls drew tight and she elected to press her point. "I'm an understudy to become a full DA myself one day."

"Hm. No need for tone, now." Ednice waved it away with a small, dainty swish of her hand. "It's just hard to stay on top of these things when certain parties never visit. Never write."

Blucille grabbed her elbows and turned her chin up and away. "Well, that's a two-way street," she quipped, keeping up her string of mumbles.

"How did the recent mass conscription play out for the two of you?" Ednice went on, unfazed. "Any more careers I should know about?"

"None for me, regrettably," Blucille answered shortly.

Ednice turned back to Art. "How about you, Mr. Mallard? It couldn't be that you have an exciting second job to speak of?"

He nodded, recovering a morsel of confidence. "A second, yes. *And* a third."

Blucille's eyes bulged wide open. She slowly looked over at him. "Say what?"

"Oh yeah. I'm triple-employed now."

"You too, huh?" a quiet voice from down the table asked.

They all turned to Redna. "You have three jobs?" Blucille was the first to inquire.

Best she could, she fixed her tired eyes on her sister. "Yup."

"On top of the countless children?"

She nodded. "Uh-huh."

They all struggled to run the numbers. "When do you sleep?"

Redna shrugged. "Some day, I hope."

They were all too uncomfortable to pursue the line of conversation any further.

"So what's this about *your* third job, Art?" Blucille pivoted. "I know you got picked up as a copy editor."

"Yup, there's that. But I've also got this other job now where all I do is collect a paycheck every week."

Ednice stopped short with a small cube of meat on the end of her fork. "Did I hear you right, just now? You're saying your job is to simply get paid?"

"That's right," he confirmed. "Simple, but it *does* contribute to the percent-employment. And hey, it's taxable income, so there's that."

"Oh," she replied, seemingly at a loss. But finally, she found an angle of attack. "Well, I'm sure it's just a pittance, anyway."

"Ha! Not hardly," Art answered. "I'm making a boatload at it! Piles and piles of cash."

"I see..." Ednice reluctantly obliged him. She shifted in her seat. "So, you evidently have quite the high opinion of your own affluence, Mr. Mallard."

"Oh, I'm a breadwinner, alright. I've got more dough than I know what ta do with."

"Hmph," Pileser put in, ruffling his paper. "I bet the Inquisition would know what to do with it."

Blucille suddenly pushed up from her chair. "This is stupid!"

Art tried to wave her down. "Now, Blucille – we agreed we weren't gonna go about it this way."

"Nope. I've already had more than enough." She glared at both her parents. "If you people want nothing more out of life than my misery, then fine. Whatever. But I won't sit here and let you pick Art apart like this. He may not always be the brightest, but he's a very hard worker. He's loyal, and dependable. He never gives up. And by golly, he has a *heart*, which is a lot more than I can say for either of you. A *lot* more." She looked at Art, wiping away angry tears. "So go ahead," she went on, resuming her onslaught. "Ruin my life a second time. But I'm not going to dress this whole charade up anymore. And I'm not going to let you pretend like this is because of any shortcoming on Art's part. He doesn't deserve that. But apparently, you think I do. You don't want me to be happy."

Finally, they were softened. "Oh, Honey..." Ednice sympathized. "It's not that we don't want you to be happy *at all*. Just not *very* happy. Do you understand? Happy people are bums. They slough off. They're so busy daydreaming that they ham-hand everything they do. And where does that get them? In an early grave, usually. It makes them a danger to themselves, and worse: a disgrace to their families. Why, just look at your sister. We let her marry who she wanted – that dull 'Jeffrey Tutankhamen' who works out of the broom closet of Ferreter and Finklestein. And now, she's a complete train wreck."

"*Thanks*," Redna muttered.

"We protected you from the mistake you were making with Bob," Pileser explained further. "You two were so taken with each other that you lost sight of what life's really about. *Work*."

"Is that what you think?" Blucille challenged them. "That I'm too immature to balance my professional life with a personal one? Do you have any idea what the workload is for an ADA in a massive city like St. Argonsburg? It's no picnic. But I've stuck it out for years now. And I've done some of my best work since Art and I started dating."

"That's right," Art agreed, getting up and standing next to her. "Mr. and Mrs. Blucille's Folks," he began, "if there's one thing ya don't have ta worry about, it's your daughter's work ethic. She juggles so many cases sometimes it's just scary. So scary it's downright adorable." He set a hand on her shoulder. "Truth is, Blackforest is darn lucky ta have her aboard. And I think he knows it."

Ednice and Pileser exchanged a look – discussing silently amongst themselves – while Art and Blucille held their breath.

After what seemed like forever, Ednice returned to them, shaking her head. "I'm sorry, Blucille. You make a good case for it. Really, you do." She shrugged. "But... right now, all we have to go on is the word of two lovebirds. You say you've got it all together. But how can we be sure?"

"How...?" Blucille started to protest, when she was suddenly cut off by the sound of knocking at the front door. Each person in the room searched all the others for some clue as to who would be calling now. None seemed to know.

KNOCK KNOCK

They all removed to the parlor to greet the newcomer.

Ednice opened the door. "Hello?"

Standing on the stoop with his bobby nestled under one arm was a police cadet, whose eyes immediately darted to Blucille before retuning to Ednice. "Sorry, Ma'am. Cadet Stallone, SAPD. I'm afraid I have to ask Assistant District Attorney Cordon to return to Headquarters with me immediately."

At the same moment, Art and Blucille met each other's gaze with sly smiles. "Excuse me, Cadet," Blucille called out. "Did I just hear you say that I'm needed quite urgently?"

"Yes, Ma'am. Right now, if not sooner."

"That's *so* interesting," she replied, slow and smug. "Could that be because I'm very important?"

Cadet Stallone's brow furrowed. "I suppose you could say that."

"Indispensable, even?"

He shrugged. "Virtually."

"Because I do first-class work, right up to the present day?"

"Of course." He looked around nervously. "Can we go now?"

"What's the situation, Cadet?" Art pried.

"It's the serial jaywalking case."

Pileser blanched. "You mean, Left Foot Lazarus?"

"Yes." He quickly returned his attention to Blucille. "There's been a development. We just arraigned a suspect – a man named Adam Oppenheimer."

Art whistled. "Horus called that one."

"Adam called it first. Funny how he knew it would come to this. I have more than a sneaking suspicion we've caught our jaywalker, whatever his shoe size suggests."

"Well, we like to think so," Stallone rejoined, pointing over his shoulder with his thumb. "We really need to get on the way. Investigator Mallard is welcome, of course."

"Yes; let's get going." Blucille gestured out the door. "After you, Art."

"Don't mind if I do," he said, sauntering out with pep in his step.

Blucille grabbed the handle and turned back into the house just as she passed the threshold. "Sorry to cut this wonderful reunion short. I'd love to stay and argue about our professional mettle, but Art and I have the biggest case in the city to crack."

Chapter 5

Captain Alexei had always been a slender man. One of the many oddities of making the switch to big city life was learning how this put him at a significant handicap in the field of law enforcement. As he stared down what should've been a very appetizing lunch – a heaping helping of gallimimus stew with extra-extra parsnips – he recalled the advice of Lieutenant Bolger, shortly after his transfer. 'A cop's got to be able to trust his gut,' Bolger had explained with upraised finger. 'That's why we eat so many donuts.' He'd patted his portly belly for emphasis. 'More gut means more to trust. And believe me, in this line of work, you want all the assurance you can get.'

Unfortunately, neither the sage wisdom of the lieutenant nor the dreamy fragrance of herbs and salted meat could inspire more than a few bites in the present moment. For over a month now, Alexei's gut – however small – had been sending him strong indications. Indications of something foul. It wasn't indigestion... even if he was suffering a chronic loss of appetite. And it wasn't trapped gas. It was just a *feeling*. One he couldn't quite put into words. One he wasn't yet prepared to acknowledge for how incredibly familiar it felt.

Reluctantly, he forced down one more parsnip before pushing the bowl away. He'd probably never have the advantages of Lieutenant Bolger... and more than ever, he was willing to accept that. At the moment, he only hoped his gut was small enough to be wrong.

Abruptly, his office door opened, and in walked Captain Huxley. "Pardon me, Sir," he said.

Alexei rose from his desk. "You must learn to stop calling me that, Huxley. We're both Captains now."

"Yes, Captain."

"What do you have to report?"

"Ms. Cordon has arrived."

"Very well," Alexei replied, tugging out his uniform as he came around front. "Show her in, please."

Huxley had only to open the door a little wider. "Hello, Captain," Blucille said as she whisked into the room.

"Hello, Ms. Cordon," Alexei replied. He held out a hand at her as she angled for a seat by the doorway. "Don't plan on getting too comfortable, now. I suggest we take this briefing on the road."

"Are you sure?" She pointed past him at the desk. "You're welcome to explain while you eat."

He looked back at the bowl momentarily. "No, that's quite alright. I've had enough for now." He began to march for the door. "Right this way, please."

* * *

"I have to say, I was relieved to hear you'd thrown the book at this 'Adam' person," Blucille said as they wound through the halls of the Civil HQ building with customarily quick, purposeful strides. "He struck me as awfully sketchy for just an innocent bystander, right from the start."

Alexei furrowed a brow at her. "You've met him already? I should like to know how. You were out of the office when we brought him in – both the first and second time."

"Well, unfortunately he managed to track Templar down to the engagement party and enlist his representation. I was there for the whole chat."

Alexei's look of intrigue changed to relative astonishment. "Most interesting. I'm not sure I like how that bodes. But at any rate, I suppose it's well that you already have a sense of the man. It'll soften some of what I have to tell you, I should hope."

More than what he said, Blucille found herself dumbfounded by their trajectory. She pointed back over her shoulder, concerned. "Alexei, we just missed our turn to the detention area."

"I know," he said gravely. "You won't find what you seek there, I'm afraid, Ms. Cordon. I'm taking you to forensics instead."

She gaped. "But why wouldn't I...?"

Suddenly, her words escaped her as both she and Alexei were stopped dead in their tracks – momentarily stunned. Up ahead of them, an entire squad of soldiers came gusting down the hall, forcing several surprised SAPD functionaries to all but leap out of their way. Leading the charge was none other than Dante Amadeus – the High Constable – whose surly expression perfectly heralded their aggressive advance.

Breathlessly, Alexei watched them all march by him while he fought his every instinct to simply let the Constable and his men go without a word. But finally, duty overcame his fears, and he called out. "Lord High Constable! I beggest thee thy pardon, Sir! We did'st not anticipate thine arrival!"

"That was kind of the point, Captain," Amadeus replied, never breaking his stride.

For his part, Alexei scrambled to stay within speaking distance. "Pray thee thou whether I, thy servant, might in some way assisteth thee?"

"You can darn well mind your own business," he called back, just as he reached the shadows of what was truly one of the department's darkest halls. "This is between me and Blackforest."

* * *

Hamilton Blackforest scratched his way a little deeper into the endless vortex of his paperwork, when suddenly there was an urgent knock on his door. In no mood to deal with any hipshot melodrama, he resolved instantly to let whatever emergency had just arisen work itself out. "It'll have to wait; I'm busy now," he called.

The door burst open. "Surely not too busy for me," Amadeus said, showing himself in.

Blackforest found his feet rather quickly. His eyes darted between the stalking form of the High Constable and the horrified secretary still standing in his doorway, apologizing wordlessly. He nodded her dismissal, turning his sharp snout and ears to face off against Amadeus' square, jutting chin, narrow eyes, and grim, protruding lip. "High Constable," Blackforest said, trying not to sound like he was asking a question.

"So this is a bad time, is it? What a shame."

The two of them circled the room – Blackforest moving to quietly shut the door, which the secretary had been too worked up to remember to close herself – Amadeus redeploying to claim Blackforest's seat.

"What can I say?" Blackforest replied, his hackles still prickling. "We're in a season of crime."

"One I trust is drawing to a close." Amadeus pulled up to the desk. "I heard you finally caught up with that jaywalking menace."

"So it seems."

"I hope and expect that's what all this is for," he said as he picked up a hearty stack of Blackforest's papers and let them slide back out across the desk. "You gearing up to throw the book at this joker."

Blackforest grinned right through a brief bout of lockjaw. "Actually, I'm not even touching the case. It's being left in the capable hands of Blucille Cordon."

Amadeus settled back in the chair, interlacing his fingers. "You're passing a case like this down to one of your ADAs?"

He shrugged. "Why play to his celebrity by handing it myself? Wouldn't it be better to treat the matter as purely routine?"

The High Constable bobbed his head thoughtfully. "There's a shrewdness to that. Very well." He leaned over the desk. "But that begs the real question. What *has* Hamilton Blackforest been doing with his time, lately?"

Just when things had apparently begun to sail smoothly, Blackforest found himself right back in the crosshairs. "That sounds more like an accusation than a question."

Amadeus reclined a second time. "Alright. Let me tell you what you've been up to. I'll start with another leading question. Does the name 'Eleven Christopher Snorkel' mean anything to you?"

Blackforest could hardly believe his razor-edged ears. He declined to answer for what apparently struck the High Constable as too long a time.

"Come on, Blackforest. The infamous pirate-admiral? Toast of the Tophtheran navy, for all its brief and dubious acclaim?"

He cleared his throat. "It rings a bell."

"Oh, I can well imagine the alarm bells are sounding." Amadeus grinned a mean-spirited grin. "You see, a strange matter has just come to my attention. The little matter of this." He produced a document. "An intelligence report shedding light on the supposed whereabouts of said pirate-admiral. A report that apparently saw some circulation around the offices of the SAPD. Which would be all well and good, except for one thing."

When Amadeus neglected for some moments to continue, Blackforest reluctantly urged him on. "And that is?"

"I'm glad you asked. Here's the strange part. As chance would have it, our friends in the navy recently passed a similar dossier on to me." He produced a second document. "Of course, Jast-Madiir has no personal beef with Snorkel – fugitive and renegade that he is. But then, there are more interested parties – parties that might pay handsomely for a good lead."

Again, the High Constable paused, forcing Blackforest's input. But by now, the futility of any further artful dodging had pretty well set in. "I don't suppose you mean the likes of the Toefthaeran Foreign Minister?"

Amadeus snapped his fingers. "Bingo. So let me ask you: What was a good and faithful servant of our dear Czarina – such as myself – supposed to do, if not make a sincere attempt to sell the information for a fair price? I sent a lieutenant to strike a bargain with the Minister. But wonder of wonders: He barely made it to the Minister before a police sergeant had the audacity to try and arrest him. Well, needless to say, it was a contentious situation. One that in the end was only defused when it was learned that the key details of the report that *my* man was there to sell and the one *your* man had apparently been instructed to *prevent* being sold didn't even match." He paused a third time while his elbows kneaded the mahogany beneath them. "Do you know what I think this all adds up to?"

"Tell me."

"I think the details of your report were dreamt up right here, on this desk. I think you fabricated information with high market value in a very niche market so you could entrap a would-be broker in your own department. The only part I don't understand is: why? *Why,* when I personally disposed of your mole problem would you *dare* go behind my back and concoct a sneaky trap like this?"

Blackforest could only turn up empty palms. His throat was dry, and his tongue was on fire, knowing his next words could be his own epitaph. But there was nothing left except to answer the question with the best-dressed honesty he could muster in the moment. "Well, what can I say? It seemed the only thing I could do to follow up on the matter personally. As District Attorney, my duty is to the integrity of this department. I didn't think it wise to spare any certainty."

Amadeus stood back up. "Your first and only duty is to do what I tell you. You've been in the game much too long not to know that by now. But seeing as my instructions alone haven't been enough to excuse your curiosity, let me give you something else to think about." He pointed at the window. "Get over here and have a look."

Confused, Blackforest nevertheless obliged. But when he reached the window, he could find nothing outside except the ordinary, everyday scene of bustling commuters. "Alright. What am I supposed to see?"

"That we're standing on a house of cards, Blackforest," Amadeus prefaced. "Do you have any idea how much confidence those little people down there lost in us when one of our own sold us out? When it took so much time and effort just to catch up with him? Can you even imagine what would happen if they got the idea that we still weren't *sure*? That maybe we've bungled things so bad that the traitor's still in our midst at this very moment? That we can't match wits with him... or even this 'Left-Foot Lazarus', who seems to live for nothing more than to make a mockery of us? Your job – my job – even the Czarina's throne itself – all depend on the people's *belief*. Their belief that we're in charge. We lose that, and we might just lose our heads. People need order in their lives, and if we can't give it to them, they'll turn on us. It wouldn't be the first time. Now, sure, we could handle a few upstarts. Dozens... even hundreds of them if we had to. But at the end of the day, we can't hang them *all*. There's just too many of them."

The High Constable's closing appeal left a bad taste in Blackforest's mouth, but he certainly made his point. He could smell Amadeus' fear, and it was infectious. "I understand."

"Good." Amadeus went for the door. "Then the case of the Brocksmith betrayal is closed. And I mean *closed*, Blackforest. All the little people have to remember who's in charge around here. And today, that starts with you."

Blackforest nodded. "You're in charge. I won't forget."

The High Constable turned the handle. "And I won't miss a chance to remind you."

* * *

Horus fairly careened through the halls of Civil HQ, energized by that special joy that arises when some outrage one predicts ahead of time comes to pass. "Make no mistake, this will certainly be another landmark case for us, Deborah," he said.

"Yes, I think you mentioned that," she replied. If her enthusiasm was somewhat less than his, he didn't notice.

"A prominent affair, and an important one... if not particularly difficult to sort out. We'll be put up against deep prejudices, of course, but the facts are as plain as they come. It should be a simple matter to prove his innocence."

"I wish I was as optimistic as you are."

He grinned at her. "Well, of course, Ms. Cordon will undoubtedly have her say, but..."

"Horus!" they heard Art call out from far off. "Horus," he repeated as he reached them. "You're not headed for the detention area by any chance, are ya?"

Horus and Deborah exchanged glances. "Well, yes. Of course. You must've heard: Adam's been arraigned."

Art nodded. "I know that. But Horus - you're wasting your time going down there. Adam's been..."

"Well, well, well, if it isn't Horus Templar," another voice intruded. They all turned, only to be quite surprised to find High Constable Dante Amadeus on approach. "Written any good speeches lately?"

"High Constable," Horus acknowledged him, far from pleasantly surprised. "None that spring to mind, I'm afraid."

"Don't be modest," Amadeus said, joining them with a wily curl on the end of his big lip. "I bet you're drafting the opening statement for the Left-Foot Lazarus trial even as we speak."

Horus blinked, looking at Blackforest, who had come up in the Constable's train. "I didn't know my choice to represent Adam Oppenheimer had already reached the upper echelons."

Amadeus shrugged. "Call it an educated guess. A case like this has you written all over it."

"So you *are* his attorney?" Blackforest demanded. "*Already*? Well, isn't today just full of wonderful surprises?"

Abruptly, Amadeus' eyes fell on Deborah. "And you must be Ms. Deborah Boulevard," he intoned. "None other than the most famous Secretary in the world." He offered his hand. "How nice to meet you in person."

She accepted his handshake with flawless diplomacy. "High Constable Amadeus. Your reputation precedes you, as well."

He smiled. "It occurs to me, just now: A Secretary of your renown is really wasted on a plebeian Public Defender... even one as formerly useful as your boss. I wonder why you shouldn't be working for someone of suitable importance."

Horus' heart skipped a beat or two. He watched silently as Deborah corralled her teeth into a grin. "Well, that's kind. But I'm really quite happy with the work I do now."

"Ah, happiness," Amadeus said airily. "An ephemeral thing, at its best." He looked back up at the DA he'd brought with him. "Wouldn't you say, Blackforest?"

"Why... I hardly know the meaning of the word," Blackforest awkwardly agreed.

Amadeus checked his pocket watch. "Well, I really must be off. But perhaps the two of us could discuss the possibility of a palatial promotion some other time, Ms. Boulevard?"

Deborah shrugged. "I... I suppose we could..." she laughed nervously.

"Very good." He nodded to all three of them in turn, ignoring Art. "Until next time, Horus... Mr. District Attorney."

As he walked away, Horus, Deborah and Blackforest only watched, trying to remember how to swallow. "That was..." Horus began.

"A thinly veiled threat?" Deborah completed his thought.

Horus nodded. "Something like that, yes."

"I guess that's just our High Constable for you," Blackforest boded. "Always happy to give a friendly reminder who's boss."

Gradually, Horus snapped out of it. "Well, reminder or no, we have our business." He turned to Blackforest. "Sorry, Hamilton, but I'm off to see my client."

"No you're not," Art cut in. "That's what I was trying to tell you, Horus. He isn't here."

Horus' brow furrowed. "What do you mean? Where is he, then?"

"On his way to find you, I suppose," Blackforest grumbled, massaging his head. "Would it surprise you to know your sweet and innocent client posted his own bail?"

"He...?" Horus started, quickly finding nowhere to go. Art and Deborah both looked back at him with doubtful expressions. "Well... that is a bit strange," he admitted.

"Sure is," Art agreed. "Horus... your client's loaded. Funny he didn't mention anything about it last night, don't ya think?"

Horus studied him blankly, trying to catalog all the logical fallacies put into play in one short sentence. "No. No, that's ridiculous. I mean, what bearing does unlikely affluence have on anything?"

Art shrugged. "Just seems kinda fishy ta me."

Horus sighed, referring to his own timepiece. "Be that as it may, I guess I'd better get back to the office right away. At this rate, I'll hardly have time to confer with him before it's back to painting Nokkaeru's house."

Deborah winced. "You're painting her house?"

Horus only gave her a defeated look.

"Long story, I take it?"

"I don't know, actually," he replied. "She offered an explanation, but I refused it."

"Well, either way, you really ought to get a move on," she said. "I'll stick around here for another hour and see what I can drudge up about the case they're building. That's about all the time I can spare before I'll have to be settled enough to do *my* other job. The clock's ticking down till I have to watch it again."

"Sounds like a plan," Horus said, before turning his attention to Art. "Art, you should come with me," he invited him. "I may yet need your help."

Art smiled nervously. "Well, gee, that sounds great and all. But I've gotta think of Blucille. She might need the city's best PI in her corner, too."

"She has the whole police department at her disposal," Horus reminded him. "Come on, Art. How better to mark your engagement than with a little professional rivalry?"

Art maintained his tightly-drawn-back look of reservation, until at last he seemed to realize he had no way of backing out. He groaned and slumped. "Alright. I guess whatever."

Horus smiled. "Glad to have your full support, my friend." He waved Art alongside him as they all started on their way back out of the station. "Speaking of Blucille, how did the meeting with her parents go?"

"Well, ya know, I'm not sure. But honestly, I think it turned out pretty good, in the end."

Horus slapped his shoulder. "That's just what I like to hear."

* * *

Miloje's face was stone. Even stonier than usual, perhaps, as he watched the motionless carriage with quietly raging indignation. There it was – parked illegally in front of the SAPD's fire hydrant. It didn't particularly matter to Miloje that the carriage was the personal conveyance of his royal superior, the High Constable, whose surprise appearance presented another aggravation – one he was content to push away for the time being, with the party in question being mercifully absent. It also didn't particularly matter to him that there were small clusters of soldiers milling about all around the carriage, where they could handily disagree with him if he dared to make a fuss. Yes, as it became increasingly clear to Miloje just how much none of this particularly mattered to him, he was left with only one recourse to his silent, brooding vigil. It was time to get in there and make a fuss...

He started his advance. Far from being intercepted by any of the troops, everyone he met eyes with looked at him with apprehension. Many even took a step back. Miloje didn't suppress a self-sure grin. Apparently, the military hadn't entirely lost a healthy respect for their civilian counterparts. Or at any rate, a healthy respect for his own projection of authority, which was just as gratifying.

As he neared the large carriage, there was a flash of motion from the back... and possibly even the bottom... of the cab. It was enough to stop him in his tracks and make him wonder. But by the time he paused and focused, there was no sign of anything out of the ordinary. One of the horses shifted, and nickered. Then nothing.

Dismissing it, Miloje took one more step before his field of vision was filled with flashing ivory teeth, and his nostrils overwhelmed a musty, putrid rot. To his most unhappy amazement, a towering serpentine mass of bone-white fur had materialized before him in the blink of an eye, hissing deadly threats with its immense throat. Frozen instantly, Miloje had enough presence of mind to appreciate how unfazed he must've seemed by this savage suprise to the outside observer. Really, though, he was presently too stunned to remember how to move.

"Easy, Stella," a husky voice addressed the beast. On command, the pale monster slinked back and down to all-fours, revealing none other than Lieutenant Carbine as he stepped out of the carriage on heavy boots, looking sickeningly pleased with himself. "We aren't here to make a mess."

"Well," Miloje scoffed, as his words returned to him. "I more than half expected to find *you*, holding the reins of this blatantly mislaid vehicle. But this... *creature*... as well? You are one for pulling strings."

His beast slithered back up on its hind legs and accepted a scratch under the chin. "She's a dire ferret, Miloje. As fine a pet as any a man could ask for."

"Oh, yes – she suits you to a tee. A weasel for a weasel."

Carbine's grin didn't even crack. He just went on petting his giant killer rodent. "You know, I enjoy these talks of ours, old man."

"You must, since you never miss an opportunity to incite them. You can't park here!"

"But I already have." He looked Miloje square in the eye. "What are you going to do about it?"

Miloje's mustache worked about contemptuously. "I wonder where you get your gall from. Obviously, you believe the High Constable will protect you from the consequences of your actions. Never mind that your predecessor – who served his master with an ardor you clearly wouldn't understand – was rather suddenly replaced one day."

Unexpectedly, Carbine's face hardened. He took a step forward. "I serve my master with deep devotion. Much more so than you serve yours with."

Miloje recovered a bit of his own amused expression. "Funny how it sounds like you're talking about two different people."

Carbine sneered – shook his head. "Someday, one of us is going to push the other too far."

"Yes, I believe you're right. And when that day comes, I'll be ready for it."

He scoffed. "Oh, really? What makes you think so?"

"I have ten reasons nigh at hand," Miloje crowed. He held up his left index finger. "One for you." He held up his right index finger. "One for your pet." He wiggled such fingers as he had left. "And eight in reserve."

Carbine appeared ready to say something especially nasty in return, when the voice of the High Constable intruded from up the steps. "Carbine!" he called out. "Our good work is done here. Let's get back to the Palace, shall we?"

"There, now," Miloje chimed, waving the big scary man away. "Be a good servant and do as you're told."

Carbine glowered, baring his teeth. "Until our fateful meeting, old man."

Miloje nodded. "I await it with great anticipation."

The Lieutenant whirled around and returned to the carriage.

Miloje basked in the glory of his verbal jousting for only a moment, until he was rudely interrupted by another up-close-and-personal snarl from Stella, who was in his face and gone again with spine-snapping speed. Finding his smile had been instantly replaced by a shell-shocked frown, Miloje resolved that once he got moving again, he would investigate the regulations for or against keeping dire ferrets as pets. Doubtless, Carbine would feel no more bound by such permissions than he supposed he was by any other known law. But at the very least, it was one more thing Miloje was confident he could add to the man's quickly-growing list of sins.

Chapter 6

"What in the name of...?" Horus remarked, momentarily unable to think of any suitably bewildering name as he struggled to make sense of the sight. Far as his eye could see to his right, the train to which his office car belonged stretched on. Given his car was customarily in the back, that much was not at all extraordinary. What really got him was the way it stretched all the way to the *left* today as well. Furthermore, as he shielded and strained his eyes to search up the mountain – where the rails wove through and over the most precipitous creases of Mt. Norvein – he could find no exposed track whatsoever that wasn't covered in cars.

"*Wowser,*" Art said, sharing his amazement. "What happened to your train, Horus? Where... where does it even end?"

"It doesn't," Gord explained, approaching the two of them with a great big rectangular parcel under one arm. "You'll remember I told you they'd be working on the railway, Horus. Well, this is it: the first ever closed-loop freight train – brought to you by Leight and Bustead Shipping Alliance – 'where our name is our guarantee'. Quite the grand experiment, I think. Imagine it: Something or someone can be loaded or unloaded at any point along the track, any time – provided he, she or it is moving fast enough. Oh, sure, unloading at the *intended* stop anywhere near on time is a bit of a logistical nightmare for now. Not to mention getting this thing going and getting it stopped again had been an impossible game of fits and starts. Still, every great innovation gets off to a rocky start. I think they'll pull it off yet."

Horus ran a hand over his ears. "Another of the new Royal Comptroller's ideas, no doubt. I hope for everyone's sake the railway crews can get this sorted. But what am I supposed to do in the meantime? I don't even recognize any of these cars. My office could be anywhere around the mountain."

Gord looked at Horus, then at Art. "I already made my suggestion."

Horus also looked at Art, who put up his hands. "Hey, now... I'm not sure about this. Ecre Point *was* supposed ta be a secret. It's bad enough Blucille convinced me ta use it as a *venue*. Next thing ya know, you guys'll have me putting in a revolving door."

"Adam already knows where it is." Horus shrugged off his reservations. "We're infinitely more likely to find each other there than here, and I'm sure he's figured that out by now. Please, Art. It's just one more case."

"I can't wait till I hear that for the tenth time," Art quipped. He took a breath, slumping. "Okay. Let's go."

"Excellent. I really appreciate it, Art. Almost as much as Deborah undoubtedly will." Just as they readied to depart once again, Horus turned back to Gord. "I, uh, suppose you're coming too?"

"Of course," Gord affirmed with a nod.

Horus eyed his parcel. "What do you have there?"

"I'm bringing my work with me," Gord explained. "My understanding is Art's secret place is underground. Not the most likely place to find windows." He patted the package. "But not to worry. I'll bring my own."

"Who is this guy, anyway?" Art asked.

"A compulsory new employee of mine named 'Gord'," Horus answered. "He muses out my window for me so I don't have to anymore."

"That's cool," Art said, giving a thumbs-up.

"It's a convenience I'll endeavor to get used to," Horus commented. He took a step back and pivoted, inviting them to follow. "Come on, now. I've been one step behind my own client long enough."

They all resumed the journey – Art hanging back a few paces to talk to Gord. "So, you must think a lot, eh?" he asked, greatly interested.

Gord nodded. "As much as any Thinker you're likely to meet."

"Neato! Any big ideas lately?"

Gord stroked his chin. "Well, just this morning I noticed this big dead animal that'd been cast off the tracks while they were bringing in more cars."

"Mm... I like where this is going already," Art said, patting his tummy. "What about it?"

"Well, it was covered in flies, and I got to thinking what a life it must be for a fly... eating off of things literally millions of times your size."

"Dreamy, for sure."

"Yes. So much so that my current muse is a whole theme park comprised of one massive cheeseburger."

Art blinked. "A cheeseburger the size of a theme park? Isn't that kinda impractical?"

"Of necessity, yes, or everyone would be doing it." He gestured profoundly. "Imagine it: Food you can get lost in. It's beautiful, really."

"Well, that depends, I guess," Art mused.

Gord questioned him with his eyes. "Depends on what?"

"On whether or not you'd cook the thing."

Gord's brow furrowed only slightly while he kept his gaze in the thoughtful distance. "I admit: That's not a question I entertained."

"Ya know, it's funny you should bring it up, though," Art segued. "Lately I've been working on this one book about a kid who gets swept off ta sea in a giant grapefruit..."

Horus only shook his head, unable to avoid overhearing it all, even if he'd really wanted to. As inane as the conversation was, he found himself enjoying it. It was a dynamic time in the city of St. Argonsburg. He had a worthy task ahead, and the people closest to him were in high spirits. Rather than be aloof about it, Horus was feeling pretty peppy himself.

* * *

When at last they reached Ecre Point, Horus and Art quickly discovered that Deborah had preceded them. They found her sitting outside the warehouse on a swanky little stool, conspicuously watching her watch as they walked up.

"Okay, we get it: we're late," Art sighed at her. "Did we really make ya that impatient?"

Her eyes didn't rise from the timepiece. "No, nothing like that. I'm just doing my job."

"I'm intrigued to know why you've chosen to do it out here," Horus said. "Are you watching for us, or for Adam?"

"For you." She pointed over her shoulder with her thumb. "Adam's already inside."

Horus nodded. "Excellent. What a relief we haven't missed each other a third time."

"Yes – very fortunate," Deborah muttered her agreement.

Horus eyed her quizzically. It suddenly occurred to him: Adam was inside; she was outside. And after all, he wasn't completely oblivious. "You know, I can't long shake the feeling you're less than enthusiastic about this case." He looked at Art. "Both of you."

Deborah shrugged apologetically. "Sorry, Boss. I'm sure it's nothing, but... honestly, your client just kind of rubs me the wrong way."

Horus truly didn't follow. "Why, whatever about him?" he chuckled. "Surely you must have a *reason* for feeling that way."

"Well, he came looking for *you* in the first place, didn't he?" Art jumped in. "That's super sketchy all by itself. Most people avoid Public Defenders like the plague."

Deborah pointed at him excitedly. "Yes; I'd thought of that too!"

"And how about that eyepatch?" Art asked her with equal enthusiasm. "I mean, when was the last time you could trust a guy with an eyepatch?"

Deborah's smile dimmed. "Well, you lost me on that one."

Horus shook his head. "I think you're both blowing a few minor abnormalities way out of proportion. Maybe he's not your favorite person. Maybe he makes a poor first impression. But even if he was the most abrasive man in the world, at the end of the day, he still couldn't have done it."

"It's not that we're saying he's *guilty*, Horus," Art assuaged him. "Just that he's kind of a creepo. That's all."

"But what if he *could* have done it?" Deborah asked abruptly, arresting their full attention. "What if the SAPD already found a way?"

* * *

"A shoe on a stick?" Adam marveled. He spent a few moments looking off in disbelief before he resorted to resigned laughter. "Well... so much for the art and subtlety of a criminal mastermind. It's bad enough being framed up for all these atrocities. Now they want to pass me off as a cheap trickster to boot."

"But it's not a question of what they want to 'pass off'," Deborah said, fists resting on her hips. "The fact is, they *found* a shoe on a stick. In a dumpster... by the crime scene. It's not a lame hypothesis. It's real. I've seen it myself."

"But that doesn't mean *I* did it!" Adam insisted. "That means anybody with an arm could've done it! Why is it still *me*? Just because I was there! How would they know someone else didn't use it?" He paused a moment as he seemed to arrive at an even more uncomfortable question. "They didn't find it until the day after. How... how would anyone know if the evidence is even... well... real evidence?"

"Excuse me?" Deborah challenged. "Are you really accusing the St. Argonsburg Police Department of fabricating evidence? They would never!"

"Darn tootin'!" Art put in. "What kind of a woman do you think I'm gettin' married to, anyway?"

"Everyone, calm down," Horus said, fair but stern. "Obviously, this is upsetting, but we have to keep our heads." He turned to Adam. "Now, first of all, it merits being said that in all my years of trying cases against the State, I have *never* seen Blackforest's people falsify anything in court. We have to focus on refuting their evidence, not their character."

Adam sighed. "You're right. I'm sorry. But it's still just so unfair! What do they have to tie me to this stick?"

"They have a witness that says he saw you ditch it on the run," Deborah revealed.

Adam sat down, cradling his head. "This can't be happening." He looked pleadingly at Horus. "Don't you see? Can't you see it now? I *am* being railroaded! It's a lie! It's a bold-faced lie!"

Horus searched Adam's eye intently. He felt certain of what he saw – a man in earnest despair. But he also had to consider his friends. They were duty-bound to help him, just as he was already bound to represent Adam to the best of his ability. Even so, stealing glances at their expressions of great doubt, he couldn't help wanting to ease their minds. Unfortunately, there wasn't much he could do in the moment. It came down to Adam's word against some unknown witness. Seeing no recourse, Horus seized on the only thing he could...

"Would you swear to that?" he asked. "Would you swear you had no prior knowledge – no connection whatsoever to this stick?"

Adam nodded emphatically. "I swear it! I swear by the Dianodes themselves."

Horus didn't relent his searching look. Though he'd long since come to terms with the moral conundrum of *forcing* the truth out of his own client, still he exercised enough of his insight to be satisfied the truth was being given to him here and now. "Alright. If what you've told me is true, it can be proved. To that end, I'll do all that I can do."

"Oh, thank you, Mr. Templar! Thank you!"

"But Horus..." Art almost whispered. "You don't really believe that...?" He couldn't seem to finish the question.

"That Blucille conjured all this up?" Horus spelled right out, only to dismiss it with a shake of his head. "No, I most certainly don't. But we have to consider there may be other parties who stand to gain from deception here... not least of all the real Left-Foot Lazarus. In any event, it's our duty to look into it. And I believe we can do it without passing premature judgment, either on Adam or the State."

Art appeared encouraged by this. "Alright, Chiefy."

Deborah sighed. "I'm sorry. To you especially, Adam. I owe you the benefit of the doubt, and I haven't given it to you."

"I'm sorry, too," Art added. "Sure, you've basically been calling my lady a no-good dirty lying cheat, but that doesn't mean you're *all* bad."

"I offer my apology as well," Gord said, keeping his keen gaze on the window he'd hung on the wall.

"For what?" Horus asked. "*You* never said anything injurious."

"Perhaps not. But I just might've been thinking it."

Adam nodded with a grin. "That's alright. Apologies accepted."

Horus clapped his hands together. "Well, why don't we get to work, then? Let's start with something simple, if we can. What do we have right in front of us to go over?"

Deborah produced a stack of papers. "I have Sergeant Basil's statement. He was the officer on duty at the time of the incident. Blucille's certain to call him up first."

"Alright," Horus replied. "Let's see what we can do with that."

* * *

"I remain confident it'll be enough to lean into the Sergeant's initial impression," Horus decided, after a few hours of reading, rehearsing, and subsequent strategizing had already whirled by them, and during which he had occasionally plucked a few notes on the piano at which he'd chosen to sit. Immediately following this very comment, he strung together a short series of airy, affirming chords.

"Alright," Deborah responded, flipping to the next in her long series of pages. "Next up she has three eyewitnesses, all prepared to say they saw Adam flee the scene after the whistleblower called out to get the Sergeant's attention."

Horus struck discordantly, raising a brow at Deborah. "That's rather alarming. Why didn't you mention it before?"

She turned up a palm. "Actually, even at my most skeptical, I didn't attach much significance to it. There were *ten* witnesses in total, and only these three picked Adam out of the lineup. None were very sure of themselves. It was a dark night, and a long street."

Horus smiled. "Well, it's little wonder how we'll answer that, then. Good work, Deborah."

She smiled back. "Thanks, Boss."

"And if I don't miss my guess, that should about wrap things up for day one in court." He executed a quick sliding scale down the keys. "Even if Ms. Cordon has time to call her star witness, I'll simply move to recess afterwards, so we can spend some quality time scrutinizing that 'shoe on a stick'."

"Hot dang," Art intoned. "The evil magician was under the fez cap the whole time!"

Everyone turned to look at him. "Come again?" Deborah invited him.

"Oh, uh, sorry," Art said, closing and holding up a thick manuscript. "Nother book I'm supposed ta edit. *Henry Poptart and the Lantern of Vague Misgivings.* It's pretty good, honestly... although I'm worried it might be controversial. But hey, a good editor can always find a back door for these little snafus. I figure, if the author just takes out all the parts that mention *magicians*, we'll be squeaky clean, no problem."

"Well, it seems some of us have already progressed to other business," Horus said, once again punctuating his own statement with a meandering little jingle. "Regrettably, it won't be long before I have to do the same."

"Did I hear music in here?" Blucille asked, coming in the door. "Well, look at that! Horus and Deborah are in! And... *oh*..." Her face promptly drew back.

"Hello," Adam squeaked, looking very much the part of the hypsilophodont in the headlights.

"Sorry to surprise you, Blucille," Horus offered. "My own office is, uh, missing in action. We've been building our defense here."

"Well, this does make things rather awkward," Blucille admitted. "I was just going to enlist Art's help, and maybe go over some strategy myself."

"Eh-heh," Art laughed, grinning most uncomfortably. "Funny thing about that, Snapfish. I kinda already ended up on Horus' side."

Her eyes bugged. "Oh, Art – you couldn't have!" she groaned. "We were going to work this case *together*! It was going to look so good for my parents!"

His shoulders crowded his head as he made his apology. "Well, ya know, technically we're still working it together. Just as enemies." He strained to think of any further good spin he could put on it. "Maybe it'll show 'em we can handle life's little spats."

She sighed. "Well, I suppose that'll have to be good enough. What's done is done." She rallied a bit of a troublemaker's smile. "Then again, maybe so much the better. They won't be able to write me off as a lovestruck buffoon when I wipe the floor with my own fiancé's best defense."

Art pointed at her with a cool look. "You're on, Sweetheart."

"Two lovers, working opposite sides of the bench. Who will triumph?" Horus narrated, playing a whole dramatic tune.

"You're very good on that thing, Templar," Blucille said with an appreciative nod. "What else can you play?"

"Depends." Horus threw down another melody. "What do you want to hear?"

Blucille raised a brow at Art. "You know, between all the formalities and the... unexpected guest... I don't believe the two of us ever got around to dancing last night. Did we, Art?"

"Sounds like something we should remedy," Art said, while the two of them drew in towards the middle of the floor.

"Play us a salsa verde," Blucille fired over her shoulder at Horus.

"Your wish is my command," he replied, before he commenced to put the keys through their paces.

Needless to say, Art and Blucille were impeccable dancers. Of course, hailing from the ranks of Mesomelae, they were preternaturally predisposed, since nary a single member of their species was ever known to be a *bad* dancer... and if it was ever so, history was quick to forget about it. Still, Horus watched them with amazement. Blucille spun and stepped in time; Art drew back and did that one especially classy move – alternatively pointing at downward and upward diagonals. It was a grand spectacle only rivalled by the sonic brilliance of his own playing. Though to him, the music was nothing – a rote task that didn't demand any real effort. He hardly noticed it, himself. Nor did he manage to notice as Deborah approached him. Not until she set a hand on his shoulder...

"You know, I think you still owe me a dance from cousin Victoria's wedding," she said.

Suddenly, Horus' piano-playing demanded utmost effort, while he tried to restrain his heart from leaping out and plucking the keys itself. "Well, uh... yes. I suppose I do at that." He looked down at his own fingers, then back up with a nervous chuckle. "Unfortunately... I'm not sure what I can do about it at the moment. My hands are rather tied."

"Allow me," Gord said, approaching the piano.

Horus winced at him. "You?"

"Yes," Gord replied – with simple, invincible confidence. "Oh, it's no trouble, Mr. Templar… you'll see. I'm classically trained."

Before Horus could further convey his doubt, he was swept from the bench as Gord seamlessly took over. He could only watch with dumb disbelief for a few long seconds, until Deborah gently elbowed him.

"There you go, Boss. I'd say you're covered."

"Wow," Art said, extending a thumbs-up as he and Blucille whirled around. "You've got it, window guy!"

"That's kind," Gord said. "I'm really better known for my adagios. Care for a change of pace?"

"Go for it."

Again, Horus' palpitations were such that he might've objected, but there simply wasn't time. Gord immediately moved onto something soft – something riding that impossibly narrow fence line between the sublimely happy and sad – but something that, in any event or interpretation, was *slow*. He watched as Art took Blucille's hand in his and set his other on her waist, knowing he would have to do the same with Deborah some time in the next century, and possibly much sooner if he didn't want to appear like a total clod-head.

Finally, he worked himself up to the task.

He took her small, elegant hand and led them on the floor – first through one little circle, then another. He couldn't help wondering what his leadership looked like to the outside observer – whether it appeared half as much like a whale trying to balance on the end of its nose as it felt like. "You know, I always meant to cut about thirty pounds before I did anything like this again," he covered.

"You're doing fine," she assured him. "You're wonderfully light on your feet."

Mercifully – maybe even imperatively – Horus was able to take her affirmation to heart and ease up a bit. After just a few more little circles, he no longer worried if he was rank with the smell of terror. A few more after that, he found he'd miraculously wandered far enough away from himself to actually *enjoy* the dance. Yes – whether by dint of his inborn talent, or the masterful playing of Gord, or some combination of both – Horus Templar was dancing with Deborah Boulevard. It wasn't impossible, or even complicated. And it was every bit as lovely as he could've hoped it would be.

"A stupid thought occurs to me, just now," Blucille said, her head against Art's shoulder.

"What's that, Snap Dragon?" Art asked.

"Snap Dragon, now?" she scoffed. "After Snapfish, and Ginger Snap... *Sugar* Snap. What's with the pattern all of a sudden?"

"You're just a snappy kinda gal," he explained in a warm voice. "But come on – what's on your mind?"

"Oh, nothing, really. Just a bit of whimsy – imagining if our big case all came down to a dance-off, right here and now."

"Believe it or not," said Horus, "the way things stand, I'd almost accept a challenge like that."

"Well, it's nice everyone can feel so at ease deciding my fate, I guess," Adam commented from the sidelines.

Horus grinned in his direction as he and Deborah went on spinning. "I'm sorry we seem to have meandered into this lighter moment without you, Adam. Particularly since there aren't any suitable dance partners to pair you up with."

"Oho, I'm sure that's just as well," Adam laughed it off, before pointing at his eye patch. "You've seen how clumsy I can be."

"The Humans have an expression for it, Horus," Blucille put in. "Call it a classic case of two left feet."

Adam shrugged. "Not a bad way of putting it."

Blucille turned her head, resting it again with her snout pointed past Art's arm. The change of angle put the other two dancers on the floor front and center. After a short while of watching them, she tsked. "Why, would you look at that?"

"Look at what?" Art asked.

"Them. *Horus and Deborah*. Do you know, I might be crazy, but they're actually kind of cute together, dancing around like that."

"Sure they are," Art agreed absently. He looked down at her. "Almost as cute as us."

Horus held his breath, bound and determined to pretend as if there was some way he could've failed to overhear them. But it was no use. Deborah looked up at him, and he knew in an instant what was coming...

"You hear that, Boss?" she asked. "Apparently, we're 'cute'."

"But of course," he covered with smooth nonchalance. "We're downright adorable."

For a long time after that, Horus and Deborah held each other's gaze. Neither really knew what to say. Neither could quite search out what the other was thinking, try as they might. But such was the thrill, and the magic of it, Horus reached a point where he found himself half-wishing Deborah could pierce the veil and read his mind. Why shouldn't she know? For once, the reasons escaped him. By now, he was just looking for it in her eyes. That flicker – that special gleam that would let him know she knew. And if he didn't find it soon, maybe he would just have to tell her.

He was ready to say it. He was really ready...

Then, the song ended... and the spell regressed. And much as he strove to hold it back, he felt logic and practicality whelming him on all sides. The silent struggle between the rational and the emotional threatened to split him in two, right there on the dance floor. *No, you fool!* he silently screamed. *You can't do it again! You **can't** back out...*

"Deborah?" he asked gently.

"Yes, Horus?" she replied, just as soft.

"I..." he battled with himself just to articulate. "...I have to go paint Nokkaeru's house now."

She seemed to take a while to process all this information. "Alright," she finally said.

Blucille checked the time, and sighed. "I guess I'd better get going, too. Lots to prepare for tomorrow, and no one here I can really prepare with."

Art gave her a congenial nod. "Okeedoke. Sorry you came all the way out here for nothin'."

"No matter. It wasn't a total loss." She turned and waved Horus to the door. "Come on, Horus. Duty calls."

Keeping his outward composure, Horus tore away at her prompting. He was much too disgusted with himself over what he was walking away from to have any idea what he might be about to step into.

* * *

"Allow me," Horus said, working the uncooperative door to the warehouse open.

"Thank you." Blucille passed through into the cool dusk.

For a while, even though they walked together, they were worlds apart, with Horus openly ruminating. Vaguely did he consider she might wonder why he was so deep in thought, and even more dimly did it seem to matter. But for all his apparent concentration, he formed little in the way of actual thought. The only thing he could really do was stew in that unrelenting sense that he blew it.

"Looks like we're headed in the same direction," Blucille interjected at some point.

"Yes," he agreed.

More silence followed.

"Well, obviously you don't want to talk about it," she said.

"Of course I don't. We're not even supposed to."

"I don't mean about the case."

Horus froze in his tracks. His ears and eyes fixed on her intensely. "What do you mean, then?" he dared ask.

"I mean, you and Deborah."

Well, needless to say, this really stopped him up. But of course, it wasn't the first time someone had guessed he might have deeper feelings for Deborah. He knew all he needed was a calm, coherent rebuttal. "I... I don't... what about...?"

"Horus, I *have* eyes. That dance was special to you. Don't pretend it wasn't."

Even cornered, he hesitated. "You and Art suspect that...?"

"I don't think Art suspects a thing," she explained, shaking her head. "After all, he's only a Detective."

Horus frowned. If he couldn't be coolly dismissive, perhaps he'd fare better with feigned indignation. "Well, maybe a Detective would know better than to see what isn't there." He started on his way again.

She caught up with him, begrudging just a few moments' peace. "It's alright. I get it. You just don't want to deal with it. It's so much easier to close yourself off. To be detached. Avoid all possible disappointment."

He stopped again, groaning. "Why do you insist on hounding me about this... this special interest in Deborah you allege I've developed all of a sudden?"

"Because I don't want to see you make the same mistake I made," she answered serenely. "Believe me, I know what it's like to be scared. Too scared to try. But Horus, think about it: fear might be the *only* thing holding you back."

Horus remained speechless. She'd given him a lot to process in very short order, and he had to admit: every bit of it sounded right on target. Denying what she had to say was fighting a losing battle. Having objectivity on her side, and life experience to boot, she seemed to understand his issues better than he understood them himself. Finally, he sighed his surrender. He even chuckled at his own expense. "Is that it? I mean, is that really all it's been, all this time? Am I merely afraid, and I've allowed myself to rationalize it a hundred different ways?" He turned a searching look at her. "Is that what I am, Ms. Cordon? Am I really just a coward in love?"

She shrugged. "You might be. But you're also one of the bravest people I know. Who else would stick his neck out for half the people you do? You've challenged the system. You've frustrated the Czarina's plans, more than once. That all takes incredible courage. Which is why I'm saying: don't let this thing beat you. There's really no point."

In the end, Horus couldn't help but smile. Nothing so filled him with dread as the possibility of being suddenly found out – particularly since the last time it happened. But Blucille was nothing like Nokkaeru. She wasn't treating him like a fool, or his troubles as something to laugh at. She was... supportive. *Encouraging*, even. "You're an extraordinary woman, Blucille Cordon. Art's incredibly fortunate he found you."

"Not half as fortunate as I am. If he hadn't, I'd still be hiding behind anything I could put in front of myself. But I'm here to tell you: It doesn't have to be that way, Horus. You can take a chance on love and actually come out on the other side."

Even as she built him up, another question threatened to tear him back down. "Do you... do you really think she'd...?"

"I think it's possible. But there's only one good way to find out... and that's for yourself." She slapped him on the side of the arm. "Grow a backbone! I promise you'll be glad you did."

He laughed. "I'll take that under advisement. But I make no promises of overnight change."

"Well, that's up to you, too. If you need to focus on the case at hand right now, I understand. Although, you might as well know: It isn't going to matter. I'm going to clean your clock in court tomorrow."

"I wouldn't be so sure. We've yet to see if the 'shoe on a stick' will leave your case with a leg to stand on."

By now, she was walking away, declining to so much as look back after his last comment. "One thing's for sure," she called over her shoulder. "I have evidence on my side. Sounds like all you have to work with are a few bad puns."

Horus only looked on for a while, feeling a kind of affirmation he'd never seriously considered possible – a confidence he'd never had. Blucille was living proof that love could triumph. Hers was the kind of encouragement he could take to heart. He *could* tell Deborah what he felt, and emerge the better for it. Soon enough – he resolved – he *would*...

Chapter 7

Horus Templar knew better than most that in the battle of the courthouse, the opening shots are often fired on the walk *to* the courthouse. Of a breed whose ears were formidable instruments, most of the flak he'd taken over the years had come in the form of quips and jabs exchanged between the commonfolk, the likes of which he may not have even been intended to hear. Sometimes, however – especially in the recent case of his representing Khonshu – he had considerably livelier ammunition to face. Gone but far from forgotten was the swollen eye he'd incurred from ballistic celery, to say nothing of a few other, lesser vegetable wounds that were also quite unpleasant. He was momentarily given to remember them all on a visceral level as he took his first step out the door that morning, bound for the opening day of *Adam Oppenheimer vs. The State*... or – as it was widely billed by the regular Joes – ***Left-Foot Lazarus*** *vs. The State*. Out of all the perceived public menaces he'd had as clients – Khonshu, Aphelo, and even the ex-baron Arcadian Tweed – Adam's alleged alter-ego was certainly not the least feared, or hated. The odds of encountering real violence seemed high, and it left Horus already with significant second thoughts about making plans to pursue Deborah romantically in the immediate future. He also didn't particularly relish the idea that he might be about to get the tar beat out of him. Even so, he marshalled bravely to meet the day head-on, come what may...

He was soon to discover the wages of his courage...

"By golly, that's Horace Templar," one Human passerby whispered to another.

"I think you mean 'Horus' Templar," his fellow corrected him. "It's spelled with a 'U-S', not an 'A-C-E'."

"Oh, shut up," the first man snapped back. "You're always such a wise-elbow about everything. It sounds exactly the same, doesn't it? How would you know how I'm spelling what I'm saying, anyway?"

Despite his resolve to remain totally impassive, Horus blinked. *Well*, he thought, *that wasn't actually so bad*...

Within moments, he drew up on another pair of gawkers. "Hey, look! That's the blood-sucking lawyer that's going to bat for Left-Foot Lazarus!"

"*Pfft*, sure it is. Next thing you'll tell me he's the same jerk who worked that ship-blower-upper case, and the Mantid trial."

"B...but he is! He *did*!"

"Get real, man. Like one guy would represent all the biggest louses this city's seen in decades. It's totally unbelievable! And we'd just happen to pass him on the street this morning? What kind of idiot do you think I am?"

...And shortly after that, another pair on the corner.

"Check it out. It's that serial jaywalker's attorney."

"Jaywalker?!" the other man exclaimed, recoiling with horror. "There's been a serial jaywalker on the loose?"

"Uh... *yeah*. Literally everybody's been talking about it for weeks. There hasn't been a scare in St. Argonsburg like this since the Syzygy. Where in the world have you been?"

"Working myself to death, thank you very much. Two twelve-hour jobs in a 21-hour day isn't an easy load to juggle. This conscription surge is killing me! I never sleep!"

By this time, Horus was quite astonished. The public had apparently become so overworked – so exasperated – perhaps even disenfranchised – that they almost couldn't exert themselves to attach any more contempt to him. He found himself grinning... practically bouncing on his footpads. He was only too happy to accept this as a good omen...

* * *

"Well – it's nice to see you made it in one piece," Deborah quipped as Horus approached their long table.

"Believe me, no one's as surprised as I am," he replied, setting his briefcase down. He fixed his eyes on the bench, where the presiding personality was already standing off to the side, studiously going over various documents. "Speaking of surprises... who do we have here? This case has Lionel Ramesses written all over it. Certainly, we should've had Senahktenre or Bastet otherwise. As for *this* judge... I have to admit, I don't even know his name."

"Thutmose, if you're really curious. I didn't know it myself before this morning. Not many people in our neck of the woods would. They called him over from his regular circuit in Lapisborough."

Horus furrowed his brow at this information. "Why would we be outsourcing for a judge? What would motivate a choice like that?"

"We've actually already touched on it. Name recognition."

"But that's the very thing he doesn't have."

"Right."

Horus waited, but Deborah was obviously enjoying his consternation. "Would you mind making sense of that?"

"It's all part of a broader effort to downplay the significance of the case. Blackforest's angling to make light of the Left-Foot Lazarus phenomenon – make it seem like arraigning a serial jaywalker is nothing more than business as usual. That's why he's not handling the prosecution himself, and why he ensured personalities like Ramesses didn't even get within arm's reach."

"Very interesting," Horus mused, scratching under his chin. "I wonder if that's even more telling than it seems."

"How so?"

"Well, is it just possible Blackforest knows their case against Adam is so weak, he's quietly opted to preserve the reputation of our toughest judges?"

Deborah shook her head. "I wouldn't bet on it." She nodded towards the bench. "Judge Thutmose might not be a household name around here, but his conviction rate rivals Bastet's and Ramesses'. You can be sure the Czarina still wants her victory, even if she's content to have it on a smaller stage than usual."

Horus sighed. "Well, she could never just *let* me win, could she?"

"No, I don't think so."

About the time they were concluding their banter, Thutmose closed up his binder and angled a nod at the back of the courtroom. There was an immediate stir as many in the gallery anticipated the words of the bailiff...

"All rise for the Honorable Judge Thutmose."

The entire room stood on command. Thutmose took a step further up behind the bench, paused in front of his seat, and then sat down, with everyone solemnly following his lead. "Court is now in session. Bring forth the accused."

Horus pivoted to watch as Adam was brought out. He quickly noted how few of the people in the gallery did likewise. Truth be told, it was a rather affecting sight, watching as many shifted uncomfortably, turning frightened eyes down and away from the aisle. Rather than broadcast their contempt and disdain for the supposed 'Left-Foot Lazarus' – the one who defied the state for no apparent reason other than defiance's own sake – there seemed to be a silent superstition at work... as if the mere sight of such a madman could somehow spread the lunacy. For Horus' part, he could only shake his head at their fears. If they would simply look up and see the terror in Adam's own eye, they would've learned at once that the poor man on trial was at least as unnerved as they were.

When at last Adam was near the table, Horus and Deborah got up to allow his shackled form to pass them down the row. He nearly tripped as he shuffled by Horus, who steadied him, even giving him a little reassuring pat on the shoulder, for which Adam returned a weak grin before continuing on.

When all were seated, and the bailiffs had resumed their stations, Thutmose again addressed the court. "We will now hear opening statements, beginning with the prosecution."

Blucille stood. "The prosecution waives its opening statement, your Honor," she said with practiced apathy, before quickly returning to her seat. Horus found this rather remarkable, even seeing that it fit perfectly with Deborah's assessment of the tenor with which the State meant to put on its case. *No flowery speech about what an affront to the crown he is? The silence speaks volumes.*

Thutmose looked at him. "And, the defense?"

Horus rose. His eyes flicked over Deborah and Adam as he belatedly realized his whole statement presumed the 'flowery speech' Blucille was supposed to make first. But it was too late to draft any major rewrites now. He'd just have to sell it...

"First of all, I resent the efforts made by the prosecution to sensationalize this case..." He could already feel the eyebrows rising. "...Few though they seem in the moment. Now, it must be granted: The crimes alleged against my client are indeed most alarming. But as in many previous instances, the zeal of the State to exact the penalty due has hastened – and I daresay, compromised – its judgment. Fair examination of the facts will reveal that Adam Oppenheimer is not the logical suspect, but rather, the expedient one. I implore you to banish all thought of the Left-Foot Lazarus persona, and see the *person* facing arbitration. No justice can be served here otherwise."

Thutmose nodded as Horus sat back down. "Very well. Moving on. Let the prosecution call its first witness."

Blucille marched into the center of the floor. "I call Sergeant Basil to the stand."

* * *

"That was when I found him – the defendant," Basil said, gesturing in Adam's direction. "He was lying on the ground, clutching his eye. The bandaged one, of course. It seemed he had struck a hanging sign. The lad was nearly unconscious when I reached him."

"I see. And what did you do when you found him like this?"

"Well, after a brief and rather fruitless attempt to question him, I secured his transport to Civil Headquarters. He was taken immediately to our infirmary. After he was examined and treated, we took his statement."

"Very good," Blucille said, pushing off from where she rested her arm on the stand as she turned away. "I'm finished with this witness."

"Defense may cross-examine," Thutmose announced.

Horus took his place in front of Basil, striking a thoughtful pose. "Now, Sergeant, I can't help noticing a number of omissions in your testimony. So many, in fact, I'm trying to decide which to start with. But perhaps it will suffice to expose the most glaring of all. How would you qualify the manner in which you brought Mr. Oppenheimer in for questioning?"

Basil's brow furrowed. "The manner?"

"Yes. Would you say – at the time – you were collecting him as a suspect, or a witness?"

"Objected to," Blucille called out. "The only relevant term here is 'person of interest'. It makes no difference whether the sergeant cast any suspicion on Mr. Oppenheimer initially or not."

"If it makes no difference, why object?" Horus replied. He turned back to Basil. "I'll be even more direct. *Did* you initially suspect Adam as the jaywalker?"

Basil hesitated. "No," he admitted. "At first, I didn't."

"And why not?"

The sergeant earnestly sized Adam up for a moment before making his answer. "Well, it seemed plain his feet were much too large to have made the print."

Horus grinned and nodded. "Thank you, Sergeant." He nearly turned away, only to quickly double back. "Oh, and one other question, if I may. You did mention earlier that you saw a man crossing the street – the man who must've been the jaywalker."

"'Saw' is near too strong a word, Mr. Templar," Basil qualified. "I glanced that way in passing. I didn't get a clear look. It was dark... and far away."

"I understand. I'm not asking for any minute details – features that might contrast those of my client. I merely wonder: To the best of your recollection, did it appear this man was holding something like a long stick?"

"Objection," Blucille cut in again. "The defense is referring to facts not yet in evidence."

"Sustained," Thutmose replied.

Horus was a bit surprised to see this objection carried so readily, but he was ultimately undaunted. "Alright... this time I'll try it more *general*. Did it seem to you this man in the street was holding anything at all?"

Basil pondered carefully. "I can't be sure, of course. He might've held something small, perhaps – something that could fit in the hand, or the crook of one's arm. But nothing conspicuous. Not so far as I can recall."

"Very good. My thanks again." Horus returned to his seat. "No further questions at this time."

Blucille resumed standing. "A few questions on cross. Sergeant Basil: Excepting the man's shoe size, was there anything to suggest he wasn't the perpetrator?"

"Nothing apart from his own testimony. He indicated he'd been thrown aside by the criminal as he fled. But we had nothing with which to corroborate this."

"No real evidence? No forensic cues? Faint shoe prints that went beyond where Adam lay? So much as a glimpse of anyone fleeing far ahead of you into the shadows?"

Basil shook his head. "No."

Blucille nodded. "Thank you. That will be all for now."

"The witness is excused," Thutmose said. "Call your next witness, madam prosecutor."

"I call Walter Intermezzo to the stand."

* * *

"It was just after the call rang out. I looked up and saw a man running away." Walter gazed with wide eyes at Adam, leveling a shaky finger. "And it was *him*! It was that guy!"

"Let the record show that the witness has identified the defendant," Blucille stated. "Thank you, Mr. Intermezzo. That will be all from me."

Following his cue to cross-examine, Horus exchanged places with Blucille. "Now, Mr. Intermezzo: An interesting touchstone of both yours and Sergeant Basil's testimonies has been this 'call' that rang out. You both mentioned that there was another witness who was shouting to draw attention to the crime. And I can't help wondering: Where *is* this witness? Seemingly, he saw what was going on better than anyone."

"Well, I wouldn't be the one to ask, I guess," Walter answered. "I heard him, but... once I saw the man on the run..." He shrugged. "Well, I never thought to look for the man who was calling out."

"So then, there's no chance you could look out into the gallery and tell me who this mysterious caller was? Even if he was present?"

"No, I'm afraid not."

"Interesting," Horus mused. "Perhaps I'll have to ask the Sergeant about it later." He pivoted towards Blucille. "That is, unless the prosecution would care to shed some light on this subject?"

"One moment, Counselor," Thutmose cautioned him. "I do believe you're out of order."

"It's alright, your Honor," Blucille said, just the same. "It's most unfortunate, but it may as well be admitted: The State has thus far failed to identify this 'Caller'. No one has come forward, and only the Sergeant mentioned even a fleeting glimpse of him – just long enough to see which way he pointed."

Thutmose scratched under his stoic muzzle. "You volunteer much, madam prosecutor. I wonder why."

"Well, quite simply, I don't intend to pass up a chance to get the word out: Whoever this Caller is, it's his civic duty to declare himself and give his testimony."

Thutmose nodded. "Duly noted." He turned back to Horus. "However, the defense will remember to confine himself to proper examination in the future."

"Yes, your Honor," Horus agreed, before shifting his eyes to Walter. "Let us return, then, to Mr. Intermezzo's testimony. You claimed it was the defendant you saw fleeing."

Walter nodded energetically. "Yes."

"You saw quite clearly that it was him?"

Walter's face drew back a bit. "Well, of course, it was dark out. He was really booking it, and..."

"Just a moment, Mr. Intermezzo," Horus interjected. "Normally, it's *I* who would remind *you* how dark it was – how fast the man was running – not the other way around. Could it be you doubt the certainty of your own testimony?"

"I, uh... well..."

"How positive would you say you were?"

"Um..."

"Are you, say, 30% positive?"

"Your Honor," Blucille called out suddenly. "The State is willing to stipulate Mr. Templar's figure. I have three witnesses – including Mr. Intermezzo here – who picked Adam Oppenheimer out of a lineup. Defense Counsel clearly means to advertise his awareness that an additional seven such witnesses failed to do so."

Judge Thutmose blinked. "Perhaps he does." He studied her unflinchingly for a few moments. "What possible reason could you have for stipulating to such an insinuation?"

"Call it prudence," she suggested with a slight shrug. "I could call each of my next two witnesses, and have the defense cast doubt on their testimonies one-by-one. I could weary the court with his appeals to darkness, distance, and quick action time and again. Or, I could stipulate to the findings of our lineups for what they are, and simply move on."

Horus' jowls tightened against his face. The judge might not understand what Blucille was doing, but he knew well enough for himself by now. She was playing with time. She was *skipping ahead.* He'd planned on the first day of court being largely – if not entirely – behind them by the time they arrived at the witness who said he saw Adam ditch the shoe on the stick. But now, she would have ample time not only to introduce that witness, but the shoe-stick itself. He hadn't prepared for this yet. And unless Art came in in the next few minutes with some radical new information, he was going to be flying blind into the most crucial substance of the entire case...

"Counselor?" Thutmose inquired, snapping him out of his grim prognostications. "Do you have any more questions for this witness?"

About a hundred more questions would've been welcome. Horus strained to think of even one. "No, your Honor," he was forced to admit at last.

"The witness is excused, then," Thutmose called, shifting his attention. "Madam prosecutor: a word with you, please, before we proceed."

"Yes, your Honor." She approached the bench.

As Blucille and the judge exchanged whispers, Horus returned to his table wearing the thousand-yard stare.

"Well, how do you like that?" Deborah asked in a hushed voice. "She jumped way ahead of us."

"So she did," Horus replied hollowly as he sat down. "And I don't like it very well at all."

"I don't understand," Adam put in from down the row. "What's going on?"

At once, Horus plastered on a reassuring grin. "Don't worry, Adam. The first day in court is always the hardest. Such is the expedience of the SAPD. They like to play to their advantage of already having all the information before the defense can get a good look at it. If she can't ensure I put on a weak case, Ms. Cordon means to catch me flat-footed during hers. She's hoping to introduce her star witness and best evidence as quickly as possible – before I know enough about either to ask any meaningful questions."

"But you can stop her, right? Slow her down?"

Horus could only shrug. The earnest anxiety on Adam's face stirred his sympathy. But what could he promise? "We'll certainly see."

"The prosecution's stipulation is admitted. Let the record show that Adam Oppenheimer was identified as the suspect in three separate police lineups."

Horus rose. "Out of ten, your Honor."

Thutmose vaguely rolled his eyes. "Yes. Out of ten. Let the prosecution call its next witness."

Blucille grinned as her eyes fixed on target. "I call Whiffle Caruthers to the stand."

The instant the name left her lips, Horus initiated his tried-and-true protocol of paying utmost attention to those particularly disarming first few moments when the witness makes his way to the front of the courtroom. Searching the gallery for movement, he spotted a small, scrawny man just as he came to his feet. Humans being rather small and scrawny by default, Horus couldn't help noticing how this fellow still managed to stick out among his peers. But of principal interest to him: Even the man's pathetic stature barely rivaled the pitiful gaze behind his inevitably oversize glasses...

Yes, Horus' attention was certainly captured. Such was Mr. Caruthers' discomfort that he knew instinctively there was a vital flaw in the testimony about to be given. But what could it be? He studied intensely, plying every power of insight he could draw on...

"Horus?" he heard Adam appeal to him weakly.

"One moment," he eventually replied, unsure if he answered Adam the first time, or even the second.

"Horus," Adam insisted.

"What is it?" he asked as he turned, hoping he didn't make it too obvious how much it flustered him to have his focus drawn away at this sensitive juncture.

"Horus, I know him. I know that man."

For a nugget like this, he no longer troubled about the interruption. "You do?"

"Yes. And believe me, he knows me, too. He used to be a regular fixture of my daily commute." Adam looked down, rubbing the back of his head. "He, uh, doesn't like me very much." Before Horus could inquire, he snapped back up, suddenly smiling. "But I mean, this is good, right? You can show bias on the part of the witness!"

"That depends," Horus said, apparently no more eager for Adam to get his hopes up than to despair. "First on getting the man to admit to knowing you, and then on being able to demonstrate his bias against you."

At about that time, Whiffle Caruthers was sworn in, and took the stand.

"Now, Mr. Caruthers," Blucille began. "Can you tell us where you were on the night of Maypril 2nd?"

Whiffle cleared his throat, appearing already rather hesitant to answer. "Well, I was working. District 5-E, that night."

"On duty. I see. Could you tell us your profession, Sir?"

Here, he really hesitated. "I'm, a... traveling salesman," he mumbled.

"What kind of salesman?"

Whiffle forced a long breath through his nostrils. "A door-to-door gun-show ticket salesman."

A quiet wave of chuckling worked its way through the gallery. Thutmose tapped the bench with his gavel. "Order. We will have order."

Blucille's face was notably drawn back. "I'm... sorry. I honestly never knew that was a profession."

"Yup. Every night, I go knocking on doors, and when someone answers, I ask, 'Would you like a ticket to the gun show?' Then they laugh and slam the door in my face."

"That sounds like miserable business," Blucille sympathized.

Whiffle shrugged. "I can think of better jobs. But it's a living, I guess."

"Well, so much for setting the scene," she quipped. "Returning to the night of the crime, what can you...?"

"E...excuse me," Whiffle interrupted, pushing the glasses up his face. "Excuse me. I don't know if this is the wrong time to bring it up. But before we really get into this, could we do that Witness' Rant thing? You know? Where I get to hurl as many insults as I can think of at the defendant?"

Blucille looked both surprised, and more than a little unsettled. "Well, um... technically we've already begun examination."

Whiffle was unmoved by her answer.

"But, uh, I suppose you *could*." She looked up at Thutmose, subtly pleading. "Perhaps his Honor should decide."

Thutmose nodded. "I will allow it."

Unexpected as it was, Horus was well-pleased with this turn of events. Not only could it play into a potential bias gambit later down the road, but more importantly, the Witness' Rant Clause might just buy him back all the time he'd lost. In essence, the Clause gave the witness free reign to craft a character-assassination filibuster of potentially limitless proportions. The only definite end to such a Rant was if the witness himself stopped talking, or if one of his insults was accidentally couched in non-committal language, such as 'sort of' or 'maybe' or 'kind of'. In that case the defense could impeach the insult as speculative, at which point traditional examination would resume. For his part, Horus had no intention of listening carefully for non-committal language to impeach. He'd gladly let Whiffle Caruthers rant till he was blue in the face, if he could...

"Thank you," Whiffle said, respectfully nodding at Thutmose before returning his eyes to the fore. "I'll keep it short and sweet. The defendant is without a doubt *the* most irreverent – most insolent – demented, deranged – warped, sadistic, sociopathic fiend in the history of the world."

Horus' eyes bugged. His hope of buying time had just evaporated as quickly as it appeared. And in the aftermath, one thing was certain. "Wow," Horus quietly summed it up. "He really *doesn't* like you."

"Oh-kay, then," Blucille said, herself recovering from the condensed intensity of the Rant. "Where were we? You said you were working District 5-E?"

He nodded. "That's right. I'd just wandered down an alleyway, when I heard shouting in the street, and the sound of running behind me. I'm a smallish man, you see, so I ducked out of the way almost by reflex – into a narrow space between two buildings. That's when I saw something strange."

"What did you see?" Blucille coached him.

"Well – the running man – I watched from the shadows, and I saw him toss an object into a dumpster just before he passed me."

"Very good. Please describe this object."

"It was, well, kind of a stick shaped thing. Could've been a broom handle, or a segment of a polearm. I'm not really sure, honestly. But the main thing is, there was a shoe on one end."

The gallery murmured their amazement. Thutmose was obliged to calm them a second time.

Blucille returned to her table just long enough to reach behind it and retrieve an object unsurprisingly similar to what he'd just described. "I show you now this shoe on a section of polearm, which was retrieved from a dumpster along the route Sergeant Basil indicated he pursued the suspect. Is this the object you saw cast off?"

He nodded. "Yes, that's it."

Blucille took the apparatus over to the evidence table. "I'd like this stamped as Prosecution Exhibit-A."

"So ordered," Thutmose granted.

"Now, who was this man, you saw?" Blucille pressed on, returning to her witness. "The man who stowed Exhibit-A?"

Whiffle pointed right at Adam. "It was him. The defendant."

Again, the crowd failed to contain their anxious muttering, ready to accept this as final confirmation that they were in the presence of a madman. "Order," Thutmose commanded.

"Thank you, Mr. Caruthers," Blucille said, nodding smugly at her witness. "I have no further questions."

Horus got up, feeling even more smug than his counterpart. During the brief testimony, he'd hatched a number of potential angles of attack, which – while a bit reckless – nevertheless felt promising. And he meant to begin with the most reckless of all...

"Now, Mr. Whiffle," he began.

"Mr. Caruthers, if you please," Whiffle interjected.

"My apologies. Mr. Caruthers, how do you know the defendant?"

The question hit Whiffle squarely in the breadbox. "Know him? I... I don't..."

"Objection!" Blucille called urgently. "No foundation."

"Sustained," Thutmose decreed. "That would be for direct examination, Counselor. You know this."

Horus grinned his way through the reprimand. Inadmissible as the question was, the look on Whiffle's face couldn't be stricken from the memory of the jurors. "Of course, your Honor," he replied, before turning back to the witness. "Let's start again. Mr. Caruthers, you said that the suspect fled down the path you yourself were on, is that right?"

"Uh, well yes," Whiffle replied weakly.

"But wouldn't that have put you in the path of Sergeant Basil as well?"

Horus could handily smell the man sweat. "Well, right. But as I mentioned, I'd already dived into the side alley."

"Oh, yes, of course." He puzzled conspicuously. "Still... I'm surprised you didn't interact with the Sergeant. Wouldn't it be customary to point him in the right direction?"

"Uh, n-no. He was past me before I had any idea what was happening. And by then he was already going the right way, so..."

"Alright. Even accepting you remained tucked away in the shadows the whole time in between the suspect's flight and the Sergeant's pursuit – allegedly a significant interval – I wonder why you didn't immediately report the key piece of evidence you saw discarded."

Whiffle blinked intensely. "Wh... I..."

"Your testimony could've resulted in my client's immediate arraignment, if all went as you say. So you mustn't have come forward for at least the first full day after the incident. It's the only way to account for the time Adam spent as a mere person of interest." Horus raised a brow at him. "How do you explain the delay, Mr. Caruthers?"

"Objected to," Blucille cut in. "The timing of the witness' testimony wasn't covered during examination. Mr. Templar can fill in the timeline during his own case, if he feels he must."

"Sustained."

Horus leaned on the stand. "Very well. Mr. Caruthers: You'll recall the Sergeant saying he initially ruled my client out as the perpetrator due to the considerable size of his feet, relative to the size of the print in the street."

Whiffle nodded a small, unblinking nod. "I remember."

"Very good. In that case, I have one more question, Mr. Caruthers. What precisely is *your* shoe size?"

"Objection!" Blucille exclaimed. "Your Honor, this is getting out of hand. Defense counsel is making no attempt at all to confine himself to proper cross-examination."

"On the contrary," Horus appealed. "The witness himself opened the door when he described himself as a smallish man. Why should I be deterred in learning exactly how small is small?"

Thutmose deliberated, tapping his pen. "I believe the question must be admitted."

Horus returned to Whiffle. "Well, Mr. Caruthers? What will it be? Size nine? Eight? Seven?"

"Um..."

"*Your Honor*!" Blucille called out quite urgently.

Everyone turned to look at her. "Yes, madam prosecutor?" Thutmose asked.

"I... I request an early recess."

The judge accepted this with notable disbelief. "*You* do?"

Her eyes danced a moment as she searched for just the right answer. "Yes."

Thutmose checked his watch. "Very well. Court is adjourned. We will reconvene tomorrow." He struck the sound block and withdrew.

Even having miraculously turned the entire course of things on its head, Horus couldn't help feeling a little wounded for a moment. *It's never that easy when* I *want a recess*, he thought. Still, he didn't long begrudge it. As everyone began to disperse, he turned a grin back at Deborah, only to be surprised by the expression on her own face. She was gripped in disbelief... much the same sort of disbelief as Blucille. "What?" he asked, feeling sudden uncertainty.

"Nothing," she replied. "I just... didn't see it going quite like this."

"Me neither!" Adam agreed excitedly. "You were amazing, Mr. Templar! How will I ever repay you?"

"He hasn't saved you yet," Blucille interjected, crossing her arms as she drew up beside the defense table.

"My sentiments exactly," Horus agreed. "It isn't over until the acquittal. Still, I'm surprised, Blucille. It seems you may have placed too much trust in your witness too readily."

She nodded with a frown. "I grant you that. Rest assured he'll be explaining himself at length as soon as we leave here. In the meantime, may I suggest you avoid making the same mistake with your client?"

"A fair suggestion. But I wonder: What exactly inspired you to share it?"

She looked crossly at Adam. "The two people at the center of all this know each other... *apparently*. That's sketchy any way you slice it." She whirled and marched away.

Horus and Deborah turned to Adam. His eye danced between them. After a moment, he sighed. "Look – I know it looks bad. But if you knew what this guy was like you wouldn't question it. When he has an axe to grind, he takes it to an absolutely insane level. I mean, I thought the last time was crazy, but..."

"Last time?" Deborah asked. "Are you saying he's tried to make trouble for you before?"

"Oh, yes," Adam answered with a hardy nod. "But in the end, it came to nothing. Clearly, he hasn't forgotten, though. This must be his sick way of trying to settle the score. I can only imagine how long he's spent dreaming all this up."

"What exactly are you suggesting he dreamt up?" Deborah continued. "Did he conspire with Left-Foot Lazarus to jaywalk in your area, run you down and knock you over so he could frame you?"

"Who's to say Left-Foot Lazarus was ever there?" Adam supposed. "Who's to say Caruthers wasn't the one who made the print then bowled me over?"

Horus shook his head – cradled his chin. "No, I don't think that's the best fit. Given when the shoe on the stick was found, I don't think it was even made until after you'd been brought in for questioning the first time."

Deborah looked at him doubtfully. "You really think Adam could've collided with the 'real' Left-Foot Lazarus just as a matter of pure happenstance? That this Whiffle character was just *gifted* the perfect opportunity to implicate Adam in something big, and he cooked up this stick business on the fly?"

"Why not?" Horus proposed. "If Whiffle's as vindictive as Adam says, he may have been tailing him a long time, just waiting for *some* opportunity. Patience has its dividends."

"Well, if that's the case, this is the biggest payoff for patience I ever heard of." She turned her questioning eyes back on Adam. "And what, pray tell, would inspire so much vindictiveness, I wonder?"

He shrugged. "Would you believe a simple argument over paying for a train ticket?"

She folded her arms. "Not readily."

"Incredible as it sounds, I don't doubt him," Horus argued. "It was *Whiffle* who decided it was in his best interest to keep their prior association a secret. Clearly *he's* the one who feels the need to hide something." He shut his briefcase. "But there's no use speculating why. Let's get out there and find the truth."

* * *

Shortly after leaving court, it was decided that Horus' part in the effort to delve deeper into the matters of Whiffle Caruthers and the shoe on the stick would be temporarily shelved. Deborah would meet with Art, exchange information and modify their objectives accordingly, while Horus himself took the gifted time to work in an inconvenient visit he had to make to his other workplace. It was his responsibility to check in the middle of the week if he had any new painting assignments. Seeing the opportunity, he elected to do it sooner rather than later.

Unfortunately, his timing turned out to be far from optimal. He happened to arrive in conjunction with a large detail of painters who were retained through the community service penal system. They crowded around the schedule, and even with Horus' greater stature and good eyesight, he couldn't quite make out his name on the sheet, however he dodged the many paint rollers slung over shoulders and indigo dunce caps in his way. It quickly grew frustrating, seeing that any real business the others had by the bulletin board had already given way to idle chatter. Now, hadn't he felt considerable pressure to be done and on his way, Horus might have taken a moment to appreciate the spirit of camaraderie that had apparently developed between a mixed group of near-criminals and the mentally unstable. But as it was, he decided to call out instead...

"Excuse me!" he called. "Excuse me. Can I please get a look at the schedule? I have other pressing business."

"Well mortgage my boardwalk... if it isn't Horus Humperdinck Hootenanny Templar," a gut-wrenchingly familiar voice answered.

Horus' ears swiveled first – long before any other part of him could remember how to move. Sure enough, when he finally looked over, there he was. "*Tweed*?"

"Whoa, now. I'm not sure I'm ready to be on a last-name basis... even with a fellow artiste." He held up a pair of paint brushes in front of him. "I gotta admit, though – all these enamels and can lids sure bring back the good ol' days." He used the brushes to act out a little scene, complete with exaggerated voices. "Good job, Archie. You stopped the flow of cosmic energies just in time for warble bingo." "All in a day's work, Horus. Now the grape lady can live happily ever after... in *jail*."

Horus' jowls were briefly cemented to the sides of his snout. There were just enough borrowed details that he honestly wondered if the unsettling little story amounted to Tweed's recollection of the Syzygy Killer case. "Well..." he segued at length. "I guess it's reassuring to see the community service agrees with you."

"Oh, yeah – it's a sweet gig." He came up beside Horus to whisper something sidelong. "Except the part where I have to work with all these *crazies*."

"You must feel so singled out," Horus commiserated.

"*Psht*. You don't know the half of it." Tweed shook his head at a big cluster of his coworkers. "Just look at these poor shlubs. Not a lick of sense between 'em. Not like me. I'm one of the sane ones, because flurgle-blurg joobee-joobee-joo."

Horus sighed. "Well, I can't argue with that." He made a show of checking his watch. "Even if I had the time. I'm sorry, Tweed, but I really have to speed this along." He took one step towards the schedule...

"I understand. That Adam Oppenheimer case has gotta be messing with you." Tweed laughed a truly disturbed little laugh. "Boy, out of all the looneys I've worked with, that guy was far and away the *craziest* of the bunch."

Horus found he was involuntarily in the midst of executing a dramatic slow-turn. He couldn't quite figure out why. This was *Tweed*. Why should he take anything the spastic little man had to say at face value? Perhaps it was the shock of hearing him use the name and the details so correctly. Maybe it just didn't feel like it fit into Tweed's old brand of insanity to say something like this. Or maybe it was just the kind of day he was having – a day full of unforeseeable associations. "You knew him?"

Tweed nodded. "Of course. But then again... at the end of the day... doesn't everyone?"

Horus said no more. As the others let him through, he stepped up and completed his errand, having to double-take at the schedule between quizzical glances he shot back at Tweed's abundantly cheerful face. It took great muster of concentration just to leave with the knowledge that he had no new painting assignments. Because even though he was sure he should know better, he couldn't shake a nagging anxiety about this whole chance encounter. What if there *was* a grain of truth in what Tweed said? Even a *single* grain?

Chapter 8

There are times when being a gumshoe is just a bit on-the-nose. When Art Mallard arose to greet the beautiful day and commenced to chase it out to the scene of the crime, he amused himself with this candid observation, just as he was stooping studiously over the first muddy shoeprint with a swanky magnifying glass, finding it to be nothing more and nothing less than described – a very clear, left-facing print. Later, on his way to Civil HQ, he reflected on the little trip he made out to Sauropod Street Zoo some months back, where his quest to disprove Deborah's reign of terror as a Werehuman had led to an inspection of footwear as well. This memory served to tickle his fancy, and he went on to recall the whole conversation he'd had with the manager. Art wished old Balchikhan well, and that he hadn't since turned into a treasure-crazed monstrosity...

It was about that time he arrived at the department building, there to see the latest shoe in the course of his aptly-named profession...

* * *

EFZ21-35-YT1300. TLZ-DMV-528491. FTL-1701-E. BLU-1492-BRB.

Art drummed the desk as he waited for help, faintly aware of the ambient crashing in the background as he read the markers on the evidence bins sequentially. He'd never really taken the time to notice all the alpha-numerics before, much less try to make sense of them. Just as well, he quickly decided. Even a passing effort to assign any rhyme or reason to the SAPD's filing system was making his head spin.

"Sorry about the wait – oh! Hi, Art!" Tracy Birdshot – the department's senior evidence curator – called out as she rushed in from the back room.

"Hi, Tracy," Art replied, exchanging earnest smiles with the little lady in the long ponytail and thick glasses. From day one of their association, Art had appreciated her easy willingness to let him browse State evidence without so much as a hint of passive-aggression. Even though it'd never been his own experience, he always figured department personnel would be loath and tight-fisted to let Private Investigators snoop through the clues they'd collected themselves, only to share their findings with mettlesome Public Defenders. He was always grateful for her cooperation. Grateful enough that the ubiquitous racket hardly registered. "Busy time?" he asked conversationally.

"Oh, you have no idea," she laughed. "On top of the recent spike in crime I've got this whole second job to manage now."

"You too, huh?" Art asked with some enthusiasm. "Come on – tell me about it. What's your second job?"

"Well, I conduct sleep studies now," she said with a sigh. "It's not a good fit, honestly. There's no time or place for it so I just have the test subjects sleep on the floor back in archives."

Art made a face. "How does that work?"

She shrugged. "Not well. They tend to wake up long before I get any meaningful information about how they're sleeping. But on the plus side none of them really have the time to spare anyway, so I guess it's for the best."

"I got ya. My second job grates on me too, sometimes." He reached into a satchel and retrieved a bunch of busy sketches. "Take this piece-a-work right here, now. I'm supposed ta be editing book manuscripts. I'm not even sure this qualifies."

"What is it?" she asked, wrinkling her nose at what she saw.

"Some kinda graphic adventures about a buncha vigilantes running around in colorful pajamas, fighting evil with all these whimsical powers, abilities, and personal fortunes." He gave her a searching look. "Tell me honestly: does that sound at all appealing ta you?"

She frowned, as if at a bad smell. "No. It sounds... insipid. I can't imagine anyone going in for that."

"Okay, good; it wasn't just me, then," he said, hurriedly stuffing it all back in his pack. "Anyway, I'm working the jaywalker case for Horus, if ya didn't already know. Do ya 'spose I could have a gander at the report for this infamous shoe-on-a-stick?"

"I can do better than that. I can show you the shoe-on-the-stick itself!"

Art's ears fixed in her direction. "Really? It's still in here?"

She shook her head. "Not *still*. They already brought it back. Just a few minutes ago." Tracy turned an uncertain look over her shoulder. "I've got it here somewhere." She commenced the search. After just a moment or two of her eyes darting across the shelves, she did her normal bit and started pulling bins out seemingly at random. It wasn't long before one crashed to the ground. "Sorry," she said.

"That, eh, filing system isn't much help ta you either, is it?" Art ventured.

She paused to raise a brow at him. "Filing system?"

"Yeah. Ya know. All those crazy numbers and letters."

"Right..." she laughed nervously. After a furtive glance in both directions, she approached him, leaning over the board to whisper. "Between the two of us, Art, there *is* no filing system. The numbers and letters are just to keep up appearances."

Art was rather amazed at this. "Really? You mean, all these years, you've just been flying by the seat of yer pants?"

She turned up her palms. "Seems like a cop-out to say I inherited a mess but it's true. There was a job opening for a reason. Anyway, I guess I've got the temperament and a good enough memory to hold it together. I almost always get it right by the seventh or eighth bin. Plus at least this way it's a code that can't be cracked." She went back to her work. "I'm sort of surprised you asked. No one ever notices the labels."

He shrugged coolly. "What can I say? Lately, I've just kinda been noticing stuff. It's the funniest thing."

"Must be, for a Detective." She intensified her noisy rummaging.

Art cast a questioning look down the front desk, to where there were a few bins waiting to be refiled. "Hey, uh, any chance it's right over here? You did say court just got out."

"*Daaah*," she said, slapping herself on the forehead. "Yeah, probably."

Art smiled. Score another one for the Detective who notices things.

By the second bin there on the desk, she paused in just such a way that let him know she'd met with success. "Okay – here it is. The '*shoe on a stick*'."

In a moment, she had it slammed down on the board between them. They both leaned over it with amazement. "Wow," Art said. "It certainly lives up to its name." He picked it up, examining the business end. "Still amazes me sometimes how big Human feet are."

"That's actually small for us," Tracy said. She took out the report, scanning over it. "Men's size 6. Anything smaller would be considered a kid's size."

"Huh." He moved on to paying special attention to the sole. "What can you tell me about the tread pattern here?"

She flipped the page. "It's the new rubber type. They call that system of lugs and trenches a 'ridgeway' sole."

"Does it say if there's much variation in the design?"

A moment passed as she read on. "None at all, actually. It's such a new method they only have one mold pattern for every size right now."

"*Mrh,*" Art lamented, even as he commenced to stroke his whiskers thoughtfully. "So it's not like we can just go out and find the guy with the matching right shoe."

"I'm afraid not. All the ridgeway shoes out there are going to be indistinguishable from each other."

Art's eyes trailed up. He grinned as a thought occurred. "Okay, so what about the stick?"

She pursed her lips at him. "What about it? A stick's a stick."

Art had to click his tongue at such a comment. "Well, now I'm really glad I asked. If that's the State's position, I might just get a leg up on ol' Shmoopsy-poo."

Tracy flipped another page of the report. "Maybe not. They actually have a lot typed out about it."

He tried to read for himself, but it was little use from his angle and distance. "Like what?"

"It says here the stick's part of an old polearm haft," she revealed. "The ash wood and lathe work for the grip fit the profile of what we used generations ago, before muskets pretty much became the exclusive weapon of the army."

Art considered this. "A hand-me-down polearm. That seems like a kernel of something. I'm just not sure what yet."

Tracy shrugged. "You might go to the Berlberi Clerks. Seems like they ran a survey not too long ago with some questions about shoe size and heirloom weaponry. Maybe someone actually filled it out."

"Eh, doubtful," Art waved it off. "But hey, I'll chew on it a while." He backed away, tipping his little detective hat. "Thanks, Tracy."

She grinned and nodded back. "No problem, Art."

* * *

Just as he was leaving Evidence, Art spied Deborah leaning against the adjacent wall, watching her watch. He hardly stifled a groan. "Ah, come on, Debs. I didn't keep ya waiting *that* long, did I?"

Deborah stifled a return groan as she stayed trained on her timepiece. "I already told you I have to do this. Don't take it personal." She looked up at the stroke of a quarter-minute. "Actually, I'm amazed you've already been in and out, Art. Seems like court only just recessed." She shot another quick glance at her watch. "Hm, but it's been a full 25 minutes. I guess I'll have to write that down."

"So, wait, why the early recess?" Art asked. "Can't be they already proved Adam guilty. I'm sure Tracy would'a said something."

Deborah shook her head. "It's a lot mirkier than we thought, Art. The principal witness for the State knows Adam and tried to hide it."

Art's eyes bugged. "Wow. That's kinda crazy." His brows knit at her. "Do ya think maybe we misjudged Adam after all?"

She sighed. "I don't know, Art. For Horus' sake, I hope we have. But no matter what comes to light, I just can't seem to shake this doubtful feeling I get whenever he's around."

"Some people just come off as sketchy," Art said with a shrug.

"Yeah," she replied absently, before fixing a more focused look at him. "So, what did you find out?"

He reviewed his tiny notepad. "Shoe is an unremarkable size 6 men's with the generic ridgeway sole design. No distinguishing marks. No nothin', really."

"Mm," Deborah harrumphed. "Blucille cut off her witness' testimony just before Horus would've had him reveal his shoe size. We can't even verify they match, for what it'd be worth."

"I might be onta something better anyway," Art was happy to reveal.

Her ears perked at this. "Oh?"

He returned to the notes. "Stick: archaic military polearm segment."

Deborah's face went blank. "You're kidding."

This reaction intrigued Art greatly. "What is it?"

"The witness threw 'polearm' out as something he thought the stick might've looked like. That struck me as oddly specific. Now you're telling me that's what it *is*? That's too uncanny not to mean something."

"Well, is it possible this guy manufactured the evidence?"

"We've been entertaining that possibility, yes," she answered with a nod.

"Okay, so we get a warrant. See if we can find the other half of the polearm stashed in his attic or something."

She shook her head. "If Whiffle's got any brains, we wouldn't likely find it before tomorrow. We might not find it at all." She thought on it a moment, then turned a questioning look back up at Art. "You said it was 'archaic'?"

"Yup. The military went all firearms a long time ago, ya know."

"So this polearm's got to be a family heirloom."

"Must be. Stands ta reason the Inquisition would've found it and thrown it out generations ago otherwise."

"I think I'm going to make a little trip to the Dronehood office," Deborah mused.

Art rolled his eyes. "You don't think this 'Whiffle' fella would've actually filled out that survey, do ya?"

She regarded him with uncertainty. "I don't know what survey you're talking about, but they might just have a telltale registration somewhere in their archives."

His face lit up with understanding. "Ah – I gotya. Sure ya don't want me ta check it out?"

"No, that's alright. Why don't you dig up what you can about Mr. Whiffle Caruthers himself? Hopefully we can find out how he knew Adam, and use it."

"Anything you can tell me ta grease the wheels? Did Adam say anything about it?"

She shrugged. "Only that it had to do with paying for a train ticket."

Art sighed. "That's not a lot, but it's something, I guess."

"Well, you have my permission to shake the rest out of Adam yourself, if you have to," Deborah quipped.

"Horus might not like that so well. I'll see what I can learn non-violently."

She nodded. "Thanks, Art. I'll see you soon."

He nodded back. "Catch ya on the flip-flop, Debs."

* * *

While professional snooping wasn't strictly a one-stop-shop, Art decided the best place to start investigating the person of Whiffle Caruthers was right where he already found himself. It didn't take long at all to confirm that he was right. For as it turned out, Whiffle had a file left over from past litigation, where he'd once before had a starring role in the prosecutor's case. Incredibly – almost unbelievably – the name of the defendant was even more familiar...

"Jumpin' jackalopes," Art swore by pure reflex.

"Find something interesting?" a lovely voice asked from the doorway.

Art jumped and closed the file, having been caught very suddenly in a manifold conflict of interest. On the one hand, he'd like to come right out and say, 'darn tootin',' since – for starters – he had. On the other hand, he was in Horus' employ, so sharing his findings with the prosecution was extremely bad form. But on the other-other hand, he couldn't very well lie and deny he'd made a major discovery. That would be obstructing evidence, to say nothing of fibbing to his best gal. "Can't say I didn't," he decided on. "But I can't say I did, either."

She rolled her eyes at him. "Relax, Art. You don't have to tell all. I'll read it for myself as soon as you're done."

"Heh, right," Art snickered. "In that case, I'll tell ya this much: Don't bother pulling up a chair, 'cause you'll just fall out of it when you get a load of this." He gave the file an indicative shake.

She groaned. "I don't need any more big surprises today. But, oh well. Whatever it is, it is what it is."

"You got that right, Sweetheart," he said – warmly, but still so cool. He couldn't help grinning at her there, leaning on the doorframe. She sure was cute when she was annoyed, which was often.

"What?" she asked gently, returning his grin.

"I was just thinking..." he intoned.

"Thinking what?"

"That I must be a beholder, 'cause I got so much beauty in my eyes."

"*Ugh*, you're just so dumb," she sighed, coming over and setting a hand on his shoulder. "And I love you for it." She rubbed his shoulder a while as her gaze wandered, and her smile diminished.

"So, you had a rough day, huh?" Art asked, taking her other hand in his.

She nodded. "You could say that. Everything just kind of blew up in my face." Her eyes returned to his, and they looked worried. "This isn't exactly shaping up to be the runaway victory I wanted to drop in my parents' lap."

"No sweat, Gumbo Gills. Even if ya fall flat on your face, it can only be because I did such a good job. We're a winner either way."

This seemed to reassure her. Even so, Art's eyes fell as the new trajectory of his evening suddenly dawned on him. "I thoughta something else, too, just now. I know ya don't want anymore surprises, but... I don't think there's any way I can keep our date tanight."

She shrugged it off well enough. "Yeah; that makes two of us. I'm going to be plenty busy giving my witness the third degree for the foreseeable future."

"You don't even know the half of it yet," Art laughed.

"Great," she muttered, before looking back up at him. "So, raincheck tomorrow?"

"You betcha. Or the day after, if tomorrow doesn't work out."

"Maybe by then I'll have a second job, just like you."

He scoffed. "You still want one a-those crazy things?"

"Of course. Bring it on."

"It could put our date off even longer..." he warned playfully.

"We'll find the time."

He nodded. "We always do."

"Well, until then..."

She just about reached up to give him a little goodbye lick on the cheek, when they were suddenly aware of another presence in the doorway. They turned to watch Horus awkwardly start to double-back the way he'd come.

"It's okay, Horus," Art called after him. "You're not interrupting a smooch-fest. We were just saying goodbye."

Horus cleared his throat as he returned to the doorway. "Very well." He looked at each of them. "I suppose I'm obliged to ask which of you is leaving."

"Don't worry, Horus," Blucille replied. "You can have your run of the archives with your private investigator. I'll come around again when you've gone."

He nodded appreciatively. "Much obliged, Blucille."

They watched her leave, waiting quietly for some time after. There were just enough cues for Horus to intuit Art had already found something worthy of private conference. No particular length of time later, they looked at each other in synchronous, silently agreeing the coast was clear.

"What did you find?" Horus asked.

"Just you wait and see," Art boded, handing Horus the file.

After a bit of scanning, Horus froze. "Well, how about that?" he intoned. "The bad blood runs deeper than I imagined. It's a grudge match, alright. And we've stumbled into round two." He gave the file back to Art, staring off in thought for a long interval. Too long to still be mulling over the words on the page...

"What're we thinkin', Horus?" Art felt the need to ask.

"That this might explain even more than it seems." He turned purposeful eyes on Art. "Pull the file on Adam. I'm going to look one up myself... on a dubious old friend."

Chapter 9

True enough, the many answers unearthed the night before left a few glaring questions. Even so, Horus met another bright and cheerful morning with boundless reserves of confidence. He'd already scripted a crushing victory for day two of *Adam Oppenheimer vs. The State*, the likes of which neither Blucille Cordon nor Whiffle Caruthers could hope to ad-lib their way out of. The surety of success, the dry warmth of the beautiful day, the energizing swill of a couple raw eggs, and now, the radiance of Deborah's smile gilded his long and meandering path. He met her there, on the sidewalk, having planned the evening prior to convene for breakfast. Officially, they were going to review, rehearse, and if necessary, strategize. Unofficially, he knew none of it was needful. After the eggs, he was hardly even hungry. It was an excuse – a harmless pretense to simply spend some time with her.

He wasn't honestly sure what he was winding himself up to do here. They'd caught meals together after late work nights plenty of times in the past. Breakfast might seem new enough – different enough – to make her wonder if he was... well... interested in the camaraderie for its own sake. Then again, it might not. It seemed like something he could try. Perhaps he could steadily propose more varied outings. Maybe they'd be dating before either one of them even knew for sure that's what they were doing. He rather fancied that idea, the more he considered it. No big spiel – no high-stakes proposition. Much as he tended to prize his chances to deliver a stirring speech, he began to feel that easing into a relationship would, in an ironic way, be just his style. There'd be plenty of time for a well-rehearsed soliloquy when it came time for the engagement...

Horus shook his head. He was getting *waaay* ahead of himself.

Deborah made a face at him as they reached one another. "What's wrong, Boss? You looked worlds away there for a second. Something come up since last night?"

"Uh, no," Horus chuckled nervously, at once feeling see-through. "Just daydreaming, I suppose." A calculated bluff – admitting a morsel of the truth.

"Oh? Care to share what about?" she asked innocently.

Horus nearly swallowed his tongue. So much for the bluff. "Why, breakfast, of course," he covered, still proffering an especially tiny *granule* of truth.

"I see. Must be you already have your order picked out?"

She got him again. "Not precisely. But I'm sure it's going to be delicious, whatever it ends up being." With his most sincere smile, he dared her not to call him out on how incredibly stupid he sounded.

Mercifully, she only shrugged. "Okay. Well, lead the way."

He was only too eager to gesture them onward. "Very well. Let's be off." No sooner than she started the way he indicated, he blanched, realizing his mistake much too late. "Um… hold up," he said, hanging one arm and shutting his eyes as he pointed the other direction. "It's this way."

She raised an eyebrow, but finally grinned. "Struggling a bit today, Boss?"

"This isn't the strong start I'd hoped for, to be sure," he said. And for the second time, they commenced their walk.

* * *

"So, they're drilling for a new aquifer in the old town square," Deborah said, her nose in the morning paper.

"Really? Isn't it quite odd to delve for water where there's already a sewer system?" Horus asked. Within the span of a few blocks' worth of small talk, he'd already rallied, and was back to feeling invincibly optimistic.

"Must be another wild Comptroller Thangorodrim idea," she ventured.

"It sounds like him, through and through," he agreed.

"Uh-oh – what's this?" Deborah asked, shooting a look further down the path.

Horus traced her gaze, finding a crowd of people around the entrance to *Grimey's Gourmet* – their intended destination. Worse yet, they were *Human* people. He groaned. "But *Grimey's* was one of the finest new places to eat. What could've happened?"

"A surge of new cooks since the job explosion, maybe," Deborah guessed.

Horus checked his pocket watch. "We don't have unlimited time to spare. Even if we did, I'd hate to wait only to have the food be awful."

"Well, what other options do we have?"

He considered the question bleakly, looking all about. "There's always *Gristle Grotto* four blocks down."

"Maybe we ought to at least go in and ask a few questions," she suggested. "See whether they're still serving any legacy food; ask about waiting times."

Horus nodded, even as his eyes settled across the square. "Alright. Why don't you go ahead? I think I'll work in a quick trip to the bank while we're here."

"Okay," she replied. "I'll see you in a few minutes."

"See you then," he said, offering a grin and a little wave.

Just after they parted ways, Horus found himself held up in another small group by a crossing guard. There were quite a few more of them in the city these days, given the recent crime wave. Even so, they were still a long way from policing all crosswalks, at all times. In a busy district of the inner city like this one, though, it was a sure thing to see a crossing guard. He waited while a number of the new cycles and a couple carriages were given the go-ahead.

In the meantime, he returned to his calculations. Supposing breakfast still worked out, what would happen if he skipped right over the slow, coy escalation of their outings and actually seized the initiative? For that matter, why exactly was he entertaining the idea of ramping up the time they spent together without expressed intentions? Was he still trying to maintain plausible deniability? Was it still cowardice guiding his decisions? Blucille had told him to grow a backbone. What might a little courage do?

There you go again, Horus, you artful dodger, he thought to himself, just as he took his first steps out into the crosswalk. *Why keep kicking the can further down the road when any moment could be yours*?

A moment later, he could hear a distant moaning... like a train whistle, but more sustained – more ominous. It didn't quite stop him in his tracks, but he felt his gut sink, and his mind spin up to full tilt, trying to recall what in the world a horn noise like that was meant to signify. Soon, he remembered, and it was all he could do to keep moving calmly on his way. Was there an unscheduled drill? Surely, that's what it was. He'd been in a couple since he came to the city of St. Argonsburg. This one just sounded a bit... *closer*. Still far enough away that the danger could be distant... assuming there was any danger at all. The chances against it, after all, were surely astronomical. But suddenly, it occurred to him where he was heading...

A bank...

There wasn't time left to turn around. Half the building ahead of him disappeared instantly in a swirling cloud of dust, ash, and cleft bricks. A concussive roar left him feeling like his veins were filled with concrete. Slowly, he willed himself to uncover his head – not remembering having covered it to begin with – so he could gaze at the whirlwind of leathery canvas flashing in and out of the soot and debris overhead. His ears swiveled to meet a *WHOOSH* like a whipping tree trunk. He turned and got a snapshot of the tail, covered in scales the size of his fist all the way to the frilly end, careening straight for him.

* * *

The next thing Horus knew was the sound of screaming and the stinging pungency of smoke in his lungs. His eyes blinked wide open as he drew rapid, panting breaths. How had he fallen asleep, only to awaken in this heckscape? Then it all came back in an instant.

Dragon.

For a while, all he could do was look around in thousand-yard amazement. There was nothing to see but desolation – the molten aftermath of a peaceful, unassuming morning just like any other. *How*? How could something like this just happen without any provocation? Without any warning? A rational little corner of his mind reminded him that dragon attacks happened frequently, all over the world. But this did nothing to counsel the deafening most quandary: How could this be happening to *him*?

The more he sat there, the more distinctly he felt that he was sure to return to his faculties much too late. *Too late for what*? To save himself, of course. The revelation failed to rouse him. There had to be something else. Something more urgent.

Finally, this too hit him.

Deborah...

He rolled over and launched himself up, but something unaccountable went horribly amiss, and he ended up smashing the side of his muzzle on the ground. After the stars subsided, a quick checksum revealed the cause. His right arm had given out under his weight. Looking at it, it was quickly obvious why.

With his good arm, he got himself on his feet a moment later, plagued by a moment of disorientation where he couldn't remember the way he'd come. Debris piles lay strewn in the paths around him, and the rolling smoke left major gaps in his line of sight. On unsure feet, he ascended a hill of bricks, believing *Grimey's* to be on the other side. A series of gunshots echoed through the haze. *Useless*, his uninhibited pragmatism told him. Admiring the courage of the poor fools attempting a counterattack would have to wait. In the meantime, an impossibly loud protest from the dragon made abundantly clear that they were all about to enjoy fruit of their efforts.

TH-THUMP

KRRUDGEN

The earth itself moved with the colossal beast. It was all Horus could do not to tumble on treacherous feet.

"Help!" he heard, much louder and more distinct than anything he'd ever heard beside the dragon's roars. "Help me, please!"

Horus found a woman partially buried under the urban landslide. It seemed to have only caught her by the legs, one of which was obviously in very bad shape.

"Help!" she repeated. "I...I can't move!"

He ended up having to forgive himself a moment's indecision, casting a look out to where *Grimey's* should be. What little he could see of it between whirling clouds appeared to be intact. That was going to have to be good enough. He couldn't leave someone like this either way...

AAAAAAAAAAARHHAA

CRUNCH

TH-THUMP

The woman pointed behind Horus. "L-look out!"

He turned, ducking just in time as the jagged belly of the dragon swung over him. But as quickly as the creature appeared, it danced back out of sight, performing some sort of maneuver against the unseen gunfighters.

"Are you alright?" The woman's voice returned, either a moment or minutes later.

Horus stood back up, putting on a face of resolution as his eyes met hers. "I'm going to get you out of here," he stated.

Finally, she seemed to notice the shape he was in himself. "But... your arm."

With his left arm and one quick heave, he lifted her out of the pile of rubble, much to her amazement. "Let's be going, shall we?" He fancied that he even managed a little reassuring grin.

Between the awkward action of slinging the woman over his shoulder, the strain of the sudden exertion, and the slow decay of his nervous system's suppression, he began to feel sharp pangs radiating from his ruined elbow. He blinked through a woozy spell or two, feeling some relief as he returned to level ground. But of course, even on the level, the world was still shuddering. He was still coughing in the smoke. And every throb in his arm was more intense than the last...

Finally, having only just returned to the side of the crosswalk whence he'd come, a shockwave under his feet brought him tumbling down. His reflex to catch himself with his free hand was a disastrous one. The agony left him dazed for several moments. When he returned, he pushed the woman on with what force he could muster. He unclenched his jaw just enough to instruct her, seeing the dumbfounded look on her face. "Go on. I can... see the daylight just ahead. Pull yourself out. You can do it."

"But what about you?"

He almost cursed her for making him say any more. The pressure from the pain and nausea felt like it was crushing all his insides. "I just need a minute," he claimed. "I'll be right behind you."

She was at a loss. But as he gave her one final little push, she began to crawl away.

Horus just laid there – left arm extended – right arm bent under him – riding out one implosion after another. He had to will himself on somehow. He knew if he could just get back on his feet, he could make it out of the dust cloud. Whatever happened after that went well beyond what he could plan for. Still, he had to get up. He had to get up...

And suddenly, he was on his feet, in broad daylight. But not because he'd found the strength himself. Rather, an immensely strong hand had reached in and hauled him up by his. He blinked. "Hihvnor?"

"Friend Templar – what a curious chance!" the Primary Administrator greeted him enthusiastically. "Please go and rest easy, now. We shall soon have the situation well in-hand."

With careful but stern force, Hihvnor pulled him back and away, while he took a few steps forward himself. Horus was quickly aware of a large contingent of Inquisitors rushing to get into position, their sidearms drawn. He cast only a brief look back over his shoulder, before doing what he could do hasten himself and the woman as far away from the kill zone as possible.

AAAAAAAAARRHHHHAAA

"Open fire!" Hihvnor ordered.

Horus heard a volley of electric chirping – another roar of immense rage, suddenly stifled. There were a few moments of excited confusion, a multitude of tinny-sounding jingles as the Inquisitors wound for another shot, and a brief wave of searing heat. Then, another volley. An anguished, quavering moan – a sound that somehow managed to strike him right in the softest underbelly of his heart. And finally, one more great crash, which sufficed to throw Horus down once again.

Each pang from his arm now blackened his vision. The danger had passed, but the darkness was closing in all the same...

"Horus," he vaguely heard a dear voice call over him. "Horus, hang in there. You're going to be alright..."

* * *

When next Horus opened his eyes, he was once again perplexed by his surroundings. At first, he remembered nothing more than the roar, the ruin, and the last horrible wail. But once he got around to recalling the rest, it was no longer quite so jarring to find himself on a cot in a massive infirmary tent. He looked up and down long rows of other cots, finding scenes of hope and hopelessness intermingled all around him. Emotionally, he was still numb. But even if he hadn't been, he supposed he wouldn't have known what to feel.

"Whoa! Glad to see you coming around, there, Champ."

Horus looked up blankly at the sudden appearance of a Human doctor.

"You were in pretty rough shape when we found you. Honestly... not entirely sure you'll pull through in the end, even now. But don't you worry that narrow little head of yours! We have this new method of rubbing chickens on people to balance out their humors, and..."

"Move aside, imbecile!" a voice that would've ordinarily chilled Horus' blood commanded. "Take your leechcraft elsewhere. This patient is under *my* supervision."

"Doctor Nokkaeru..." Horus said, the Heron surgeon filling his field of vision as she nearly pecked her Human counterpart out of the way. "I... I feel almost as if I'm pleased to see you."

"And well you should be," she informed him haughtily. "So also these many others. The dragon wrought quite enough havoc on its own. But had these backward people been left to their own medicine, I'm certain the collateral damage would have been truly inestimable."

Horus grinned weakly, then. "You're a great humanitarian after all, Doctor."

"And you're delirious."

He found himself looking around. "Forasius?"

She nodded. "He's here. Would *he* be kept away, if I was not?"

Horus settled back down in his cot. "No, I wouldn't think so. But then..." He paused, surprised by a sudden wash of uncertainty. "Things, well... they don't seem to make very much sense today."

"You've experienced major trauma, Counselor," Nokkaeru explained. "Psychological as well as physical. Your body will mend. But I would suggest guarding your mind. I wouldn't want it spoiled before your *true* disaster befalls you."

Horus took some exception to this remark – and not just for her little reminder of that ever-elusive calamity he was supposed to have one day, which he'd apparently fallen short of once again. She might not know it, but he'd spent years being drilled as a soldier by the Eighth Vigil of Aridos. He could handle a bit of battlefield trauma. "I'll see if I can hold myself together a little longer."

She seemed to deliberate telling him something else, just then. "There's another acquaintance of yours here, you know."

Suddenly, his iron grip on his emotions slackened. "Deborah?"

"Don't trouble your fragile heart. She's quite unharmed. She only waits for you."

He took a deep, calming breath. "Would you bring her to me?"

She sighed. "Oh, very well. I suppose I have no grounds to prevent you indulging yourself in her sympathy. Particularly if it will help speed you back into commission. You remained unconscious far too long."

He nodded. "Alright."

She departed brusquely. And before long, there was Deborah, standing in her place. Her eyes didn't offer any trace of pain or doubt. What she *did* give him was exactly what he was hoping for: a confident, slightly sarcastic smile. "You picked an interesting time to catch up on your sleep, Boss."

"I seem to have missed a few things." He shifted in the cot, lifting himself on his good arm, finally finding the other in a sling and a splint. "But no matter. I still had my fair share of the excitement."

She looked down at his arm, already a bit more serious. "They say you'll be in that rig for a month or so."

"Ridiculous," he dismissed it. "I've had breaks like this before. I don't give it a day over five weeks."

"Well, I hope a clipped wing won't make your painting work too difficult."

"Passably more difficult than it'll make lawyering."

This fetched a single laugh, before they both fell silent a while.

"What about you, Deborah?" he asked her. "Are you alright?"

"I'm just fine," she scoffed. "I wasn't in the thick of it like you were."

"Still too close for comfort, I'm sure."

Her eyes fell. "I won't lie – it was terrifying. Being on the threshold of danger, looking in... it's got its own brand of fear about it. But I guess it also has a way of making you think. Of bringing the things that're most important more clearly into focus."

Horus had no answer for that. Caught in the gauntlet of so much senseless destruction himself, his own experience had left him just trying to avoid the question of whether anything was really important at all.

Finally, she looked back up, appearing to have something quite serious on her mind. "Horus?" she said weakly.

Whatever emotional interference Horus was facing, the intent look on her face had the immediate effect of cutting through much of it. "Yes?"

She tried to begin, but stopped herself. But after taking a breath, she tried again. "Horus... I don't really know how to..."

"You fools!" Nokkaeru suddenly burst back onto the scene. "There's no time for idle banter! You have to be in court within the hour!"

Horus and Deborah exchanged an urgent look. The attack wouldn't excuse their tardiness. Whatever moment might have been, they had to let it pass. They had to get moving right away...

Chapter 10

Though he would hardly admit it to himself, the further Horus trekked along from the harrowing events of that morning, the more it seemed he couldn't really get away from it. There was just too much to process. His senses kept reviewing the moments leading up to the incident. Everything was so calm and serene, just like always. Just like it was now. And the next second...

He kept imagining he could hear the siren, still blaring just beyond earshot. He kept thinking he could feel the tremors of a beast the size of a building laying waste to a city block. Worst of all, he couldn't get past the mournful sound the dragon made as it was dying.

He knew it was all fantasy, of course. His heightened state of awareness would subside, in time. Until then, he had the powers of rationality he needed to ride it out.

Chiefly, at the moment, he felt he would have to be patient with Deborah's own agitation. Every so often along the way to the courthouse, she kept insisting they had to pick up the pace. He didn't feel any great need or desire to oblige her, but he wasn't about to press the issue. He'd goad himself along a little faster, until the next time she insisted he was falling behind...

Deborah. How different the morning could've been for both of them. He'd been winding himself up for a fateful encounter, just moments before he had one. He, and the whole city block with him. He wondered how many others had been nursing private dreams and aspirations up to that very moment. He wondered how many left loved ones behind. But perhaps what vexed him most was knowing he could've been one of them. That there was really no reason he *shouldn't* have been one of them. His part to play in the vast scheme of things was no more pivotal – his hopes and plans no more important than any of theirs. In an odd way, it made him feel childish. Childish for hoping and planning for anything to begin with.

"Horus... we have to *go*," Deborah coached him.

Forcing a long breath through his snout, he sped up again.

* * *

They reached the court without a moment to spare. Judge Thutmose eyed Horus' cast, which didn't suffice to soften his accusatory expression. Horus imagined his own face was less than friendly as they locked eyes. They'd made it in time. That was enough. Thutmose's disapproval didn't move him.

On the other hand, when he caught the look of suppressed panic Adam was wearing, Horus found himself softened just a bit.

"Horus, you made it," his client said. "I… I couldn't imagine where you were all this time. I was beside myself."

Horus and Deborah took their seats at the table with him. "Regrettably, we were delayed," Horus explained, busying his good hand with his briefcase. "I'm only sorry to have caused you any grief."

Adam shot a glance at his sling. "I guess I should ask what happened to the arm."

"Nothing that should trouble anyone again," Horus replied, his own words unexpectedly conjuring thoughts of all the people who wouldn't be troubled by *anything* anymore.

"All rise for the Honorable Judge Thutmose," the bailiff announced, as per usual.

Everyone stood, only for the time it took Thutmose to stoop down into his chair behind the bench. "Court is now in session," he announced. "We are obliged to let the defense continue his cross examination. Mr. Whiffle Caruthers will take the stand." He lightly struck the sound block.

While Horus' eyes traced Whiffle with an impassive air, his mind was secretly whirling. Everything they'd learned the night before – and practically the entire case along with it – had been tucked away in a small and surprisingly distant corner of his mind… and he hadn't even noticed until this moment. He had mere seconds to unpack his entire game plan from deep storage. Fortunately, the momentary shock of misplacing everything passed, and the relevant data steadily began to filter back to the forefront. More than that: a much-needed sense of the inevitable rightness of things started to reemerge. Because once he got going, he knew there was only one way this could go…

"Mr. Caruthers," Horus began, approaching the witness stand. "First and foremost, I feel I must offer you this opportunity to withdraw your earlier testimony."

Whiffle blinked. "Withdraw?" He forced a laugh. "Pray tell what part of it."

"The whole thing, if you know what's good for you." He set his hand on the rail between them, eyeing the little man seriously. "You are aware of the penalty for perjury, aren't you?"

"Of course. It's death." He looked past Horus to Adam. "Same as jaywalking."

"Then I urge you to withdraw, Mr. Caruthers. You've been found out. There's no use sticking to your lie any longer."

He folded his small arms. "And why would I be lying? Huh? What would make me want to come up here and risk the death penalty?"

"How about revenge?"

"Objection!" Blucille called out.

"Sustained." Judge Thutmose had another unhappy look for Horus. "You were reminded once before to confine yourself to proper cross-examination."

"Your Honor, it is my intention to show bias on the part of this witness," Horus appealed. "Furthermore, it is my hope that once his history of antagonism toward my client comes to light, Mr. Caruthers will avail himself of his opportunity to withdraw his testimony, before I am forced to expose the extent of its falsehood."

Thutmose leaned back in his seat, tapping the small end of his gavel lightly – if impatiently – on the bench. "You seem quite bold in availing yourself of every chance to call this witness a liar... albeit without having yet produced any evidence that it is so."

"If the witness would only cooperate and save himself, I'd have no need for boldness." Horus turned and looked at Blucille. "What about you, Ms. Cordon? Surely by now you've learned all that I have. Do you really want your witness to face the gallows, just to slow me down?"

"*Enough*," Thutmose commanded, employing the business end of his little hammer. "I will certainly not tolerate your engaging in personalities, Mr. Templar. The objection has already been sustained."

"Your Honor," Blucille called. She hesitated as all eyes turned on her. "I, um... I withdraw my objection."

Thutmose froze. "Excuse me, madam prosecutor?"

She needed another moment, but she rallied. "That's right. I withdraw my objection. On further consideration, I believe the defense is acting in the best interest of this witness."

The judge was not at all pleased with this. But at length, he sighed. "Very well. I've never heard of withdrawing an objection *after* it's been sustained. But if that's what you wish..." He struck his sound block again.

Horus returned to Whiffle. "Alright, now. Where were we? Ah, yes – your vendetta against my client." He returned to his desk, where Deborah handed him the rare bit of aid from his briefcase – a stack of papers to wave in Whiffle's face. "I have here the complete transcript of a case in which Adam Oppenheimer was the defendant, and you, Sir, were the principal witness. What do you have to say to that?"

The courtroom turned deadly quiet.

Whiffle rolled his jaw, silently seething. "I say it can't be all *that* complete," he tried, at last. "We're still in the middle, aren't we?"

"Closer to the end than you might like, I'd wager," Horus riposted. "But come now, Mr. Caruthers – you know better than that. I'm not talking about *this* case. I'm talking about the one before."

Whiffle had no smart remark for that. He looked bursting to say something, but nothing came out. Meanwhile, the rest of the court was silent no more. The gallery murmured its disbelief.

"The case where you accused my client of an act of vagrancy," Horus continued. "You were once a train conductor, were you not?"

A specially hot ember caught in Whiffle's eyes. "*Once*. Yes. And I was a very *good* conductor. Just ask anyone who actually worked with me."

Horus deftly flipped through his pages with one hand, just as if it was something he'd done a thousand times. "The opinions of several of your fellow employees *were* collected in this previous suit, Mr. Caruthers. The psychological profile here is of a man with a sporadic temper... and a pronounced difficulty letting things go."

"Mr. Templar," Thutmose cautioned. "Alarming as the revelation of this second case may be, don't think I'm granting you unlimited latitude here – objection or no. If you are allowed to expound that transcript, it will be for the purpose of introducing *facts*, not opinions."

Horus nodded up at him. "Yes, your Honor." He returned his focus to Whiffle. "Alright – to the facts. You were also the plaintiff in this suit?"

"Yes," he admitted reluctantly.

"You alleged Mr. Oppenheimer was freight-hopping one of your cars?"

"Yes."

"But he was ultimately acquitted. The court found no evidence that he ever swindled the railway."

Whiffle shook his head. "The courts make mistakes. You're making a big one right now."

Horus leaned further over the rail. "*Was* he acquitted? Yes or no."

The word came up like it was covered in barbs. "Yes."

"But that wasn't the end of your troubles, was it? The railway decided to distance itself from you after the failed suit. To arrange other employment for the conductor who'd stirred up a lot of legal uproar over nothing. That's how you came to be in your present line of work, isn't it, Mr. Caruthers?"

"They cast me off... like so much baggage. After all those years of faithful, whole-hearted service. I'd been given authority, and responsibility. I had pride in my work. Now I'm just a traveling joke."

"You hate your new job, don't you?" Horus ventured.

"Hate is a strong word. But almost not strong enough."

"So, then: Wouldn't you say you've answered your own initial question? Why you would falsify testimony about Adam Oppenheimer?"

Whiffle scoffed. "What? Just because he happens to be the man that ruined my entire life?"

"Well, what would you think if you were a juror? Wouldn't it appear you have every reason to hate him?"

"I *do*. I *do* hate him," Whiffle admitted openly. "But only because he earned it. He earned it once before, and he's earned it again." He pointed the finger at Adam. "That's your jaywalker, sure as death. I already said what I saw. I won't budge on a word of it."

Horus tried to stare the man down, but to no avail. Whiffle was much more stubborn than he'd hoped, or even imagined. All he could do was keep pressing the issue and pray he would still be able to give the man an opportunity to renege on his testimony before it was too late. "Alright. If establishing clear motive isn't enough to move you, perhaps a closer look at the material evidence will be more persuasive." He turned to the bailiff in charge of stamping evidence. "I'd like Prosecution Exhibit-A brought to the witness for examination."

The bailiff obliged, bringing the 'shoe on a stick' over and holding it out in front of Whiffle.

"Here we are," Horus said. "Rather remarkable in a way, wouldn't you say? Such a humble instrument with which to commit a grievous wickedness."

Whiffle looked surprised at him – even rather pleased. "You give yourself away, Mr. Templar. Even *you* admit this was used in the crime."

Horus nodded. "I do. But not the crime you'd like us to believe it was used in." He accepted another document from Deborah – the police report that went with the Exhibit. "Let's begin with the shoe itself. Size six – quite miniscule." He glanced at Whiffle over the paper. "You will of course remember when I asked you what your own shoe size was?"

"Ah, I see now," Whiffle supposed. "You're going to paint *me* as Left-Foot Lazarus, are you?"

"Not at all," Horus replied. "It may be significant that your size matches that of the shoe found here... but then again, it may not. Undoubtedly there are thousands of shoes just like it in St. Argonsburg, and nearly as many people wearing them. Even if we were to have found a lone right shoe in your possession, I'd be hopeless to prove conclusively that this shoe is yours."

"Darn straight you would be," Whiffle agreed with a nod.

Horus made another dramatic page-flip. "The stick, on the other hand, is another matter altogether."

Whiffle frowned.

"During your testimony, you described it as – I quote – 'a stick shaped thing. Could've been a broom handle, or a segment of a polearm.'" He eyed Whiffle with a raised brow. "Shrewdly chosen guesses, Mr. Caruthers. Never mind how odd it is that you could correctly identify a length of an antiquated polearm in the dark as a man scrambled to stash it in a dumpster. You knew you needed to seem quite observant, so you included the truth. It *is* a segment of polearm. But of course, you knew that. You only included the bit about the broom handle to introduce a reasonable sense of uncertainty. But you won't be able to obstruct how much you really knew any longer. You ought to withdraw your testimony now."

He shook his head. "Absolutely not."

Horus' gut sank. Every emergency exit Whiffle turned down was another step towards the gallows. The last thing Horus wanted was to be forced to save his own client at the expense of another man's life. He wavered, and stalled. But ultimately, he knew he had to continue. Because at the end of the day, his one overriding duty *was* to his client...

"Very well. You leave me with no choice but to call you out directly. You knew this was a segment of polearm because it belongs to you."

The gallery responded instantly to the scandal. Judge Thutmose had to make repeated appeals to order.

"How do you propose to prove *that*?" Whiffle challenged, when the crowd noise had died down. "Are you going to get a search warrant for my house? Turn it inside-out for the other half of a polearm? Go through my papers to see if I've got it registered? Go ahead. You won't find anything."

"No, I suspect I wouldn't," Horus admitted solemnly. "But I don't have to. You certainly could've disposed of said evidence – destroyed your *own* records. But you would never have gotten to this..."

On cue, Deborah handed him yet another paper. Whiffle eyed it as his grey face turned pale. "What is that?" he asked quietly.

"The Clerical Dronehood of Berlberi's copy of a certificate in your name. A *family heirloom* certificate. The item registered is a polearm."

The onlookers erupted again. Thutmose and his gavel demanded their silence. Whiffle only slumped in his chair, looking ghastly.

"The way I see it, you have two options, Mr. Caruthers," Horus said at length. "Produce the polearm in its entirety, and all this goes away. Or else take this last opportunity to admit you lied and avoid perjury."

Whiffle blinked up at Horus with narrow eyes. The look on his face changed instantly from terror to rage. Horus' heart skipped a beat. Even cornered, the man didn't have the slightest intention of taking his only way out. He hadn't surrendered. He'd snapped...

"No."

"Mr. Caruthers," Horus pleaded. "You have to..."

"You *heard* me," Whiffle interrupted. "I said: No."

"Your Honor," Blucille called out. "If I could be permitted a moment to speak with my witness..."

"No!" Whiffle barked, shooting up to his feet. "He won't get away with it again! Not while I'm still breathing! He *begged* me to look the other way when I found him hopping the train car! Said he couldn't make ends meet – that he had a wife and kids to feed! But it was all *bunk*!"

"Order!" Thutmose commanded, hitting the sound block good and hard.

"He would've said anything to cheat the system! And the only reason he got away with it was because I'd been stupid enough to pay his fare myself! I just tried to do a nice thing and he shamelessly ruined me with my own goodwill! You can't let him get away!"

CLACK

"Order!!"

A pair of bailiffs seized Whiffle. Everything was confusion for several long seconds as the men dragged him out of court, wrestling and hurling curses at Adam as he went. Horus was half dead to it. He didn't really watch. He only stared vacantly in disbelief.

"Madam prosecutor," Thutmose breathed. "Your witness seems to have quite impeached himself. I feel I have no choice but to recess, whereupon you *will* draw up charges against Whiffle Caruthers for contempt of court."

"Your Honor, I..." she tried.

"...Furthermore, you will enlist whatever means are necessary to learn the extent of his perjury. Only then will we have the clarity needed to continue this case in earnest... if indeed there is any case remaining in the wake of this."

Before Blucille could begin to protest again, Thutmose struck with his gavel, and the court was adjourned.

While everyone else slowly collected themselves to withdraw, Horus and Blucille remained utterly motionless at the front of the court.

"Horus, I'm a fool," Blucille said, by way of apology. "I just went right ahead and took his deposition at face value. And by the time I learned everything you did, well... it was too late to..."

"Don't blame yourself, Blucille," Deborah interjected, gaining her attention as well as Horus'. "You both gave him every opportunity to back down. It was *his* choice not to take you up on it." She turned sympathetic eyes on Horus as she came up beside him. "You're going to have to anchor yourselves with that."

Horus set his hand on her shoulder. "Thank you, Deborah. I call that sound advice." He had no intention of taking it. But he hoped with his affirmation, Blucille would.

For her part, Blucille said no more as she withdrew, holding herself up in a way that clearly took a bit of coaching. Horus and Deborah watched until she was far enough away that it felt safe to confer privately.

"Well, now what do you suppose we do?" Deborah asked.

Horus needed to give that some thought – thought that he had to keep wrangling out of the fog. "I suppose we can only keep our wits about us for now. It's not even my turn to put on a case yet. Blucille might still have a bit more up her sleeve. Though I can't imagine what."

She searched his eyes. "You going to be alright, Boss?"

He nodded – grinned. "I'll be fine." It wasn't a lie. He was sure he'd come around eventually.

"Alright. Well, I'm going to use the extra time to get caught up with my other job. I'll meet you at the office?"

"I suppose by that you mean Art's place?"

"Of course."

"Then yes," he assured her. "I'll be there presently."

She nodded, and walked away.

Much as Horus might've otherwise brooded over her departure – why he insisted on bottling-up his present sense of total exasperation, and all the like – he was quickly brought back to reality when, as he watched her go, he happened to look over and see for the first time the extravagant – even rather off-putting – expression of joy on Adam's face. It befuddled Horus in no small way. He'd been so distraught about how everything played out, he'd forgotten what a good turn this was for his client...

"You did so well, Horus," Adam told him. "I can't tell you how relieved I am. It was incredible. One question right after the other, you had that Whiffle guy dead to rights."

Horus didn't care at all for his choice of words. "Yes, well, 'that Whiffle guy' just paid the ultimate price for your acquittal. I'm glad you're relieved. I wish I could share your relief. But all I can seem to do right now is wonder *why*. Why did he stubbornly throw his life away?" His eyes were questioning. "Was there any truth to what he said, in the end?"

Adam's expression fell. "Horus... he's insane. You saw how he went off. He signed his own death warrant in a fit of rage. No one in his right mind would do what he did. What happened was... unfortunate. But supposing things had gone *his* way. He would've had me killed for nothing... and who knows how many other people afterwards? I'm sure it's hard, but you have to accept this is for the best. A crazy man like that shouldn't be on the streets."

Earnest as his answer was, Adam couldn't help reminding Horus of other questions. "You know, it's rather curious how many crazy people have shaped your fortunes."

Adam tilted his head. "What do you mean by that?"

"I found out where you got your bail money from. Not that I was looking, mind you. It was rather a chance encounter that led to more findings. Of course, following your first case, you were naturally penalized with community service for having been suspicious enough to merit litigation. It was during that community service that you met your most unusual benefactor. A one former-Baron Arcadian Tweed."

"Yeah, that Archie was an odd duck," Adam snickered. "And you're right: He was kind enough to share a little money they missed when they took his barony back."

Horus only stared at him.

"Okay, maybe more than a *little* money."

"I don't suppose you'd care to explain what inspired his generosity?"

Adam shrugged. "Who can explain what goes through a head like his? I'm sure it was just one of his wild impulses."

"Knowing Tweed, that's more than likely," Horus admitted. "Still, it's strange. Strange the way lunacy just seems to find you."

"Well, it's like I've said before. I'm always..."

"...Always stumbling into things," Horus interrupted. "Yes, I haven't forgotten. But I wonder just how many wild twists of fate can be excused that way."

Again, Adam turned up innocent palms. "I don't know what else I can say, Horus. What's a man to do if he runs into a string of bad luck?"

Whether he knew it or not, Adam's question hit home. As things stood, Horus appreciated the sentiment better than anyone. He couldn't seem to do anything right today, much less hope to explain why everything was going so catastrophically wrong instead. "Of course; you're right," he assented. "I'm sorry, Adam. It's been a rough day."

"Think nothing of it," Adam replied. "Believe me: I've gotten pretty used to being the object of suspicion. If anything, it means that much more that you went to bat for me today."

"Well, that *is* my job," Horus reminded him.

Adam smiled. "Yes, I suppose it is, isn't it?"

* * *

One can never really outpace one's own thoughts, but it's often some relief to try. Horus left the court in a purposeful haste. What the walk itself and the throbbing pain in his arm wouldn't do to clear his mind would just have to be made up for with simple mental discipline. While he marched ever further away from his second complete disaster of the day, he looked for solace in the thought that somewhere, something had to be going right for someone...

Chapter 11

"So, let's see... what else did I have highlighted here?" Art said, narrating his perusal of T.R. Winnebaker's manuscript. "Oh, yeah," he chuckled. "How could I forget about this one?" He straightened the paper, even as he straightened his own posture, preparing to quote. "'And then, they shared true love's first kiss'," he read aloud. His face drew back as he gave the author across from him a wide-eyed look. "That seems a little edgy for literature, don't ya think?"

"Well, I..."

"...But hey – not ta worry. I've got just the thing for it." He took up a pencil, making what he knew to be the perfect adjustment. "True... love's... first... handshake." He smiled a toothy smile. "There, now. Doesn't that just hit ya right in the ol' breadbasket?"

"Uh... it's fine... I guess," Winnebaker replied, sweating bullets. Art couldn't have known it, but the man was not so much horrified at the present butchering of his prose, as he was at the prospect of what Art would think when he got to the even more shocking part where the characters got married out of wedlock.

"And another thing – this *word* you keep using. And I mean constantly. Like almost every time there's dialogue."

Winnebaker blinked rapidly. He leaned on one hand. "Wh...what word might that be?"

"*Said*," Art said. "Said, said, *said*. I gotta tell ya, it gets boring after a while. Of course, it's not entirely your fault. All the other authors I've been reading are pretty attached ta 'said' too for some odd reason. But you strike me as just the right fella ta try something else out with. So, what's your pleasure? I've got a whole pack of dandy alternatives. Check it out. 'Uttered'. 'Communicated'. 'Verbalized'. 'Opined'." He looked up at Winnebaker again expectantly. "Which one da ya like?"

"Uhhm..." Winnebaker answered.

Presently, there was a knock at the front door.

"Sorry, Bub," Art excused himself as he hurried to his feet. "Other business calls. When I get back we can talk about dropping that silly pen-name-initials-thing all you writer guys are doing, too."

Winnebaker forced out a breath, wiping his forehead with a handkerchief. "I'll try to be ready."

With a flourish of innocent enthusiasm, Art whisked the door open. "*Gadzooks*," he couldn't help swearing under his breath, finding the hostile countenance of Blucille's parents darkening his doorway. "Uh-h… hi, there, folks."

They only frowned at him.

"Of course I mean 'folks' in the common sense. Ya know, like, 'Yes, sir, them's some good folks' and whatnot. I'm not trying ta call ya *my* folks. That'd sure be presumptuous. Er… not that I'm trying ta call ya *common*, either. I just meant, well…"

"Are you going to let us in, or what?" Pileser asked.

Art snickered, opened the door wider, and gestured in. "Sure thing. Make yourselves at home."

* * *

Soon, they were all seated in Art's sitting room – appropriately enough. Ednice busied herself boring holes in Art with her eyes, while Pileser took up the morning paper, having apparently come all the way out just to pretend he didn't exist. The room was altogether silent, apart from the manic drumming of nails, which Art eventually realized were his own. "So, uh, nice day, isn't it?"

"There was a dragon attack downtown," Pileser revealed from within the paper. "Flattened the whole Greensquare Bank. Sheer pandemonium."

Art could feel his teeth locking up. "Gee… that's a bummer," he offered at length.

There was another, painfully long interval of silence.

When at last it was certain the burden remained with Art to advance the conversation, he cleared his throat, which had fortunately become so bone-dry as to inspire his next icebreaker. "I've, uh, got refreshments. Anyone for a cherry soda?"

"*Hmph*," Pileser scoffed, shaking out the headlines. "A soda-drinker, too."

"We'll pass," Ednice answered.

"Cherry soda's not your favorite, huh? I get that." Art ventured, trying to at least be congenial.

"Actually, it *is* our favorite," Ednice said.

"…Oh…" he replied.

More eternities came and went without further remark.

"...Maybe just a plain ol' glass of water?" Art suggested.

Pileser folded his paper down. "Ednice, maybe we should just come to the point," he suggested.

Ednice smiled at him insincerely. "*We* could have come to the point already, if we weren't so busy with our nose stuck in the newspaper, Darling."

He didn't share her cheerful expression. "When did *we* decide that *we* had to be *me*?"

She huffed. "Alright, then – I'll start." Her renewed look of accusation fell back on Art. "Do you love her?"

Art locked up unexpectedly. It wasn't that he didn't have a quick answer. But when everything he said got turned around on him anyway, how should he respond? In the end, he could only go with what was most simple and honest. "I do."

"But do you *really* love her?" Ednice pressed him.

He nodded. "I *really* do."

She sat back, sighing. Pileser exchanged a tentative look with her. "That's what we were afraid of."

"Look – I know you guys think you've gotta moderate her happiness. That in your own weird way, you're just trying to be good parents. But I'm telling ya, if you'd just look at all she's accomplished..."

"Save it, young man," Pileser cut him off. "We've already done our homework since the last time. And as much as we hate to admit it, you're not wrong. Our Blucille was doing pretty well for herself before *you* came along. Unfortunately, it appears she's done just as well afterwards."

Art had no words. An involuntary smile came bubbling up out of him. Could it really be that the single obstacle left in their way had elected to remove itself? Because that's what it was starting to sound like...

"Now, don't get too excited," Ednice was quick to warn him. "We aren't going to go along with *anything* until we can agree on certain ground rules. If the two of you want a truly fulfilling – and dare I say, enviable – marriage, you're going to have to model it after ours."

Art's eyes swept between the dour, humorless faces of Blucille's mother and father – a wide sweep of his vision indeed, since the two were seated so incredibly far apart. "Okay, shoot."

"First of all, you have to cultivate a healthy disdain for one another. If there's anything you do that positively drives Blucille up the wall – or vice-versa – make sure to do it as often as possible."

"Petty sarcasm and passive-aggression are good places to start," Pileser advised.

"As is continuously walling yourself off behind mindless drivel," Ednice added, eyeing his newspaper.

"Which brings us to the second condition." Pileser leaned forward. "Whenever and however you can, be disengaged. Disinterested. Attention is finite. You can't afford to waste more than you absolutely have to on your wife, any more than she can afford to waste hers on you. Especially once the pups come."

"That's right," Ednice agreed. "I regret to say we weren't always such a model couple. We were somewhat closer and more affectionate when the children were small. By the time we saw what a bad example we were setting, it was much too late. Hence our present difficulty."

Pileser harumphed his accord with a nod.

Art already had his notebook out and jotting. "Okay, so let's see if I got this. You want us ta spend all our time either driving each other batty or ignoring each other?"

"I'd say that pretty well sums it up... yes," said Ednice.

"Okay, got it. Anything else?"

They conferred silently for a moment before shaking their heads. "I think that might suffice," Pileser answered.

"Well, alright," Art sighed. "I won't promise we'll stick to it, but if ya think it's that important, we can certainly try it out."

Ednice and Pileser exchanged another look, before Ednice shrugged. "I suppose that will have to be good enough. Present company proves we can't dissuade Blucille from favoring a certain type of man. But rather than hamper her endlessly, perhaps it's better to simply let her have her marriage and resolve to meddle in it the best we're able."

Once again, Art couldn't have stopped himself smiling if he tried. "Oh, thank you! Thank you so much! I mean so, *so* much! You won't be sorry! This really is the best – the kindest thing you could do!"

"Don't think us kind," Pileser cautioned him. "We're not. We're bitter, spiteful, mean-spirited people." Unbidden, there was a tiny flicker of a glint in his eye. "But... even *we* care too much about our little girl to hurt her the same way we did before."

Ednice nodded, coming over and setting a hand on Pileser's shoulder. "We had the best of intentions. I'll always stand by that. But for better or worse, it's true. We just couldn't bring ourselves to shoot her down again."

She turned her doting eyes towards Art, whence they immediately returned to drilling laser beams. "So do us all a big favor and shape up. Understand?"

Art saluted. "Abso-posi-lutely, Ma'am!" he said. "I won't let ya down. I'll be surly. I'll be distant. I'll be a big grouch. At least for a trial run. I'll..."

Suddenly, there was another knock at the door.

"...Stick a pin in that thought." Art whisked away to answer the knock. He couldn't quite tell if he was skipping, flying, or merely running as he blew through the house. He flung the door open, momentarily perplexed to find no one there. But then, he chanced to look down far enough to see the Phage postman at the threshold. "Oh, hey there, little buddy."

"Greetings, Sir," the postal worker said. "Would you happen to be Artimus Mallard, perchance?"

"Well a'course I am; you know that!" Art laughed. "I've met ya at the mailbox a dozen times, ya silly goof!"

"Indeed," the postman agreed. "Nevertheless, I am required to ask." He produced an envelope. "I have this registered letter that you must sign for."

Art took the letter. Unexpected though it was, the return address explained all. "Would ya look at that? I guess ol' Stewart Jamison's had that breakthrough he was gunning for. Boy, it must be a humdinger. He didn't even want me ta wait and find this in the mailbox."

"You are at liberty, of course, to share what you will about your correspondence, Sir. Be that as it may, I wish you would not share it with *me*. It is certainly none of my business."

Art hurriedly signed for the letter. "Sorry, Pal. Guess I do run at the mouth when I'm excited." He handed his signature off. "Here's this for ya. My thanks for a job well-done."

"No thanks are necessary. Good day, Mr. Mallard."

"Happy trails ta you, too, Buddy."

Art turned back into his house, having just enough time to open the letter and confirm its contents before Ednice and Pileser joined him in the foyer.

"What's all the excitement?" Ednice asked.

"No time to explain," Art explained. "Duty calls." He grabbed his hat and trench coat, just in case the occasion called for extra airs of professional detection. "Hey, this is great! An early chance ta put my money where my mouth is. See this, guys? I have the best news in the world ta share with Blucille, but I'm gonna give her the brush-off and go do this silly work stuff first! How's that for priorities, huh?"

"Well, it's a start, I suppose," Ednice replied tentatively.

"Great – thanks so much for coming – hope ya have a fantabular day!" Art almost couldn't recite fast enough as he rushed off, closing the door behind him, leaving his future in-laws a bit shell-shocked.

"Well, that was more enthusiasm than I needed to see," Ednice commented. "I do hope we've done the right thing."

"We have," her husband assured her. "We've been over it a hundred times. This was the lesser of two evils."

Before any further counsel could be taken, their gazes wandered off to the side, as they both became aware of another presence leaning sneakily into the room. "Is he actually gone?" author T.R. Winnebaker asked.

* * *

With great jazzy steps filled with pep, Art ate up the distance between himself and Steward Jamison's house in what seemed like no time, until only a few blocks remained. All along the way, he nodded, waved, smiled at and finger-gunned various passers-by. Their faces were of the same drab sort they always were. No doubt they were troubled by tales of a dragon's wrath, by the hardship of sharing a city with a serial jaywalker who may or may not still be on the lam, and by a truly crushing workload. But the more Art saw of it, the more his cheerfulness grew. It was like a little self-appointed mission to shake these people up and get them to see the bright side.

Turning from a bunch of pedestrians who watched him with especially pronounced doubt, he came into a wide square, at the far side of which a number of tall brick buildings huddled together in their own deep shadows. He knew that just beyond them, he would come out up the road from Detective Jamison's house.

That's when he chanced to spy something odd up ahead – a man leaning out from behind a wall, checking over his shoulder, and then dashing into the open. Art's beaming face dialed down its intensity as his brows drew together. There was something exceptionally strange in the man's gait – in his lanky shape – in the familiar, investigatory silhouette of his hat. Suddenly, Art's smile returned, realizing it was the very eccentric fellow he'd gone out to see to begin with that was currently on a beeline to him…

"Hey! Hey, Jamison!" he called out. "Fancy meeting you here! What's the big hurry?"

Jamison froze for a second, fixing crazy eyes on Art, before he took off running even faster, waving ahead of himself with reckless force. "Double back, Aart! Hurry! Get outta here!"

Art frowned. "Now, don't start that again, Jamison. Whatdaya...?"

BANG

With only a few paces between them, a wave of reflex caused everyone on the block to duck and cover their heads as a shot rang out. Art forced the quaver out of his knees and stood back up straight, taking quick stock and knowing surely he hadn't been hit. But the man in front of him – his fellow sleuth – could hardly coax himself through another faltering step. Art reached out and caught him under the arms just as he collapsed. He sat him down gently and rolled him over. A flurry of ineffectual starts and glances followed as Art lost himself in a tangle of disbelief...

"Jamison..." he finally articulated. "What did... why did they...?"

Through a face of anguish, Jamison struggled to croak something out. "I... I am..." That was all he got. He swooned, and closed his eyes.

"Hang in there, Jamison," Art coached him. "You've gotta hang in there!" He looked up, watching as people scrambled every which-way. "Help! Medic! Somebody get this guy a medic!"

To his amazement, Art's wandering eyes homed in on someone calmly approaching the scene. Someone who clearly had anything but helpful intentions. Art couldn't believe what he saw. The *gunman*... marching straight up to him, with gun still in-hand. And he wore no disguise – no false pretense whatsoever. All he had to legitimize himself was his uniform, and he clearly thought that was enough. But then, this wasn't just some random blue-coat. Art knew him in an instant. It was that scary guy from the High Constable's staff. It was Lieutenant Carbine...

Art had only just enough time to spring to his feet and turn the gun away as Carbine aimed it down at Jamison's head.

BANG

More screaming and scattering in the background. Art was speechless as he fought to keep the gun trained safely down and away. Carbine may have been a Human, but he was of a particularly large and strong variety, making the contest more pitted than Art would've preferred. His intervention earned him an immediate evil eye.

"What do you think you're doing?" Carbine asked.

"*Me*?" Art demanded. "What about you? Huh?"

"I know exactly what *I'm* doing. Let go of the gun... or you'll regret you interfered."

"No way, Pal. Military man or not, you can't just pop a guy like this."

In one quick action, Carbine let go of his pistol and stepped back as he drew another one from his arsenal. "I can 'pop' two just as easily as one if I have to. Now step aside."

Art hesitated. This was neither the day nor the way it should end for him. Indeed, far from it. But how could he just let something like this happen?

Fortunately, things were immediately taken out of his hands. Before any more words or gunfire could be exchanged, they heard several blares on a police whistle nearby. "You, there! Freeze! Put your hands up!"

Carbine slow-blinked his exasperation, before – at length – he let his gun hang from his finger, turning to the cop with his hands up. Art raised his hands as well, nearly flinging the other gun in his sudden, self-aware haste to be rid of it.

Keeping his own firearm trained in their direction, the policeman maneuvered around them to check Jamison, setting two fingers on his neck.

His examination went on far too long for Art's comfort. "Is he dead?" he had to ask.

The policeman shook his head. "No. But he soon may be." He looked up at them with a questioning gaze. "I know this man. This is Detective Steward Jamison."

Carbine rolled his eyes. "I'm well aware of that. You're interfering with a sensitive operation, Corporal. I'm going to have to ask that you remove yourself from the situation at once."

"I don't think so," the policeman replied with a curt shake of his head. "We're going to get the Detective some medical attention. Then the two of you are coming back to the station with me. You've got some serious explaining to do."

* * *

Art watched solemnly as Hamilton Blackforest walked up to Jamison's bedside. The Detective was an affecting sight, tethered to numerous strange pieces of equipment. Thin tubes full of blood ran directly into his arm from a bag that stood over him on a metal hangar. A significantly wider hose was wedged into his mouth, apparently supplying him with concentrated oxygen. At least the blood, Art could understand. Jamison had lost a lot of it. The oxygen seemed gratuitous – like they were just disfiguring his nearly-lifeless body. If it hadn't been his own pal Doctor Nokkaeru overseeing things, Art would've probably had a few choice words about it. Instead, he'd spent the last hour in an anxious silence. A silence he knew Blackforest was about to break...

"What's your assessment, Doctor?" the DA asked.

"I regret to say I don't know," Nokkaeru answered, uncharacteristically subdued. "The crux of the matter is the bullet. As it stands, he has no chance whatsoever of surviving its extraction. Precious time and blood were lost in getting him to proper care. He will need to recover his strength before any attempt can be made at life-saving surgery. But there are many variables over which I can exert little influence. He will have to remain very still, or the bullet will never stay in one place long enough to stop the internal hemorrhaging. And he will have to do it without benefit of a sedative. Chemically depressing his system might kill him outright at this stage. But even if he improves significantly, I can't be sure of anything. If the bullet is lodged too deep in his spine, there may be no hope of retrieving it."

"I see," Blackforest replied, before he nodded. "Thank you, Doctor." Soft-spoken as he was with Nokkaeru, he suddenly turned all business as his eyes fixed on Art. "Alright – now to the next order of business. Who shot him, Art?"

Art could hardly help a glance across the room at Lieutenant Carbine, who had so far suffered his internment with silent indignation. He'd admitted to nothing. Art didn't suppose Blackforest had even noticed him yet, holed up in his dark corner. Trying to prevent him from finishing Jamison off had been climbing out on a limb as it was. Ratting out a ranking officer struck Art as another gamble. "I'm not sure I'm allowed ta say," he finally answered.

Blackforest's jowls adhered to his razor fangs, showing off just a bit of his longest canines. "Excuse me? What did you say? Clearly, I misheard you. You're not sure if...?"

"It was me," Carbine admitted, standing up straight. "I shot him."

Blackforest managed to look even more displeased as he traced the sound of the voice. "*You*? What possible reason could you have for committing this atrocity?"

"Oh, don't be so dramatic, Blackforest. I was merely enforcing the strict order of the High Constable that the old business of the mole in the SAPD be left to rest. Jamison knew very well he was not to pursue the matter any further. Yet he persisted." He grinned roguishly. "The penalty should be the same for anyone who defies the mandate of the Constable. Wouldn't you say?"

No one – perhaps least of all Blackforest himself – really expected things to escalate from there. The lieutenant's implication was clear enough. But it didn't have quite the cowing effect that was intended. Blackforest marched right up on him, hackles raised sharper than a porcupine's pelt. Carbine recoiled as a shimmering nail was pointed in his face, not an inch away. "In this city, we have a little thing called due process, and it goes through *me*. If the High Constable thinks I'm just going to sit back and let him go martial law on anyone he wants, he has another thing coming. And as for *you*: You can't possibly be as ignorant as you seem. But even if you are, I'd say you've dodged accountability long enough. I'm arraigning you on charges of attempted murder and assault with a deadly weapon. And you better hope first degree murder doesn't end up on the list."

It wasn't until Blackforest backed off, and Carbine had a chance to check his face for drawn blood that the lieutenant recovered the gall to answer. The DA hadn't even touched him, but from that close range he evidently felt the prick of the nail just the same. "Do as you see fit, Blackforest. I'm sure Amadeus will be only too happy to preside over my case *himself*... in military tribunal."

Blackforest forced a breath through his snout. "Yes, I suppose he will. But in the meantime, I have just the place for you to wait and see." He looked at a pair of policemen on either side of the doorway. "Lock him up."

Carbine allowed himself to be taken away, looking more and more fiendishly amused by the time he left the room. At that point, Blackforest commenced to pace, appearing to mutter an incendiary streak. Art could hear nothing, but the vague imagination of what he was saying was enough to singe the tips of his ears. He found himself suddenly self-conscious. "Hey... I'm sorry I didn't come right out with it when you asked," he offered. "I just wasn't sure if..."

"It's alright, Art – I understand," Blackforest interjected, dismissing the apology as a mere annoyance. "Truth be told, I'm not sure what locking up and charging the High Constable's personal butcher is going to fetch me in the long run, either. But at least we'll have one more force of chaos off the streets for a while."

Art looked back down at the hospital bed. "I still can't believe it really happened. Jamison came running up to me, and that scary guy just plugged him right in the middle of the square. I was there to catch him when he went down. I tried to tell him it'd be alright."

Blackforest stopped abruptly, fixing a serious gaze on Art. "Did he say anything to *you*? Anything at all?"

Art shook his head. "He tried to. Darn, but he tried. 'I am' was all he got out."

Blackforest sighed. "Well, I don't see getting anywhere with that."

Art suddenly remembered something else – something he once dismissed as immaterial. "He had a wall. A great big crazy-person project he was working on. The names of everybody in the department, and long lists of broken phrases under 'em. Maybe he got somewhere with that... I dunno. When he showed it ta me, it looked totally bananas. But he musta thought he made *some* kinda breakthrough. He sent for me – shaved his hobo beard. All the signs are there."

"And maybe no way to decode them," Blackforest lamented. "But, alright. We'll have a good hard look at the house. Maybe we'll learn something. Assuming Lieutenant Carbine didn't get to that first, too."

There was a knock on the open door. They both turned their ears and heads to find Deputy Constable Miloje leaning into the room. "Hamilton: a private word, if you please."

"Of course – just a moment, Stenya."

Miloje nodded grimly.

Blackforest returned his attention to Art. "Thank you for your cooperation, Art. You're clear of all suspicion, of course. You may go. But I do hope you'll come back and check on our embattled Detective, whenever you have opportunity."

"Sure thing," Art assured him. "I'll be here every moment I can spare."

Blackforest nodded, and left the room.

When he'd gone, Art turned to Nokkaeru. "He'll come around, won't he, Doc?"

Nokkaeru hung her head. "Far be it from me to disappoint you, Friend Mallard. I'll certainly do all in my power to assure the recovery of your valued compatriot. But you heard my assessment. His prognosis leaves me with no clear indication of any end, whether good or ill."

"Yeah, I got that part. But what about your Heron future-seeing stuff? What does that tell ya?"

She regarded Jamison for a lengthy study. "I regret to admit: The power you speak of is not in me. I cannot see the future. However, I do occasionally feel something of its texture – of its ceaseless troubles and sorrows. There is nothing I can say certainly, Friend Mallard, nor do I lightly invoke conjecture. Yet because you ask, I will answer as best I may: I feel the greater trouble is soon to come."

Art frowned. "Well, I hope you're wrong about that."

She nodded. "For your sake, my comrade – and that of my sterling reputation as a surgeon – I do as well."

As Nokkaeru once again busied herself, Art reached out and carefully patted Jamison's shoulder. "Don't worry, Jamison. They winged ya, but we slapped a big ol' band-aid on it. You'll be right as rain in no time."

* * *

Blackforest found Miloje borrowing a dark, vacant room of the infirmary wing a few doors down, leaning back against a table by the window with his arms crossed. His face was almost totally eclipsed, but the shadow couldn't hide his steady, intense eyes. "Do shut that door, won't you?" he asked.

Blackforest quietly obliged. "Alright. Now what, may I ask, demands all this discretion?"

"On my way to you just now, I chanced to see a vision straight out of my own fancy play out before my very eyes. A particularly large and loathsome rodent being led away to a well-deserved detention. Now, perhaps I shouldn't wonder. And in fact, I fear I already know the answer. Even so, I must ask. What was it, Hamilton? What did he do that we've finally caught up with him?"

"He did exactly what you think he did. He shot Detective Jamison."

"And how did he presume to justify a crime like that, pray tell? I do hope it was cleverer than his customary excuse... which is none at all."

"He claimed to be enforcing the order of the High Constable."

Miloje shook his head – stroked his chin. "Well, now, isn't that a fine riddle? It seems that in our efforts to root out the spy in our midst, we are consistently hampered by our own beloved Constable."

Blackforest assumed his own posture of repose. "What *exactly* are you implying?"

Miloje huffed. "Come now, old friend. I no more wish to say it aloud than you do. But how long can we skirt the obvious answer? The most inconvenient answer of all? Amadeus is the sellout we've been looking for."

Blackforest shook his head. "No. Believe me, I see what you're saying, but it can't be like that. He has no motive."

"Hasn't he? What about money? We know his pocketbook has been riding lighter in his vest since the Kaiser debacle."

"But think about the *leak*, Stenya. Why would he sell the Eighth Vigil knowledge of the magic elixir he'd already promised to the Berlie Beirel Queens, knowing what they'd do with it? War profiteering is his business. You know very well he stood to take his cut of that sale. It's like taking money out of one pocket and putting it in the other."

"A fair point, to be sure. But how else can we explain the carnage he's left behind him ever since? Brocksmith – gunned down for the crime with almost no corroborating evidence. Jamison – the one fellow who might've learned the truth – now hanging by a thread for his trouble. How could it be anything but a coverup, of which Amadeus is clearly the ringleader?"

"It *is* a coverup," Blackforest assented. "But not of the kind you're suggesting."

Miloje's mustache ruffled. "Then *what* kind? What do you know of it?"

Blackforest ran a hand over his ears. "On Amadeus' last visit, he confronted me about my own attempts to draw out the mole."

The old policeman's brow furrowed. "Yours?"

"Yes. He was quite adamant that I desist."

"Why? Why is it so deadly important to him to drop it?"

"In a word: fear. Fear of public perception... not only of the department, but the entire administration. He's convinced of an existential threat to our credibility. A threat we created when our corrupt element came explosively to light, and we failed to meet it in a timely manner. A threat we'd only feed if the public caught wind of the fact that we're *still* unsure of ourselves."

Miloje didn't look greatly impressed. "And you're satisfied with that reasoning?"

"What choice do I have but to accept it? He's still the High Constable. And if we're completely honest with ourselves, we *are* looking pretty shabby these days. We must be, for as bold as the criminals in this city are getting."

Miloje sighed. "I grant that we've suffered embarrassment. Pray, let us not speak of it now, and darken our counsel yet further." His face quickly hardened again. "But for one so concerned with image as Amadeus claims to be, he should've reached for a subtler instrument than his *Lieutenant Carbine*." He hung his head, shaking it. "Such an ugly thing he did... on a day that had already seen so much grief and confusion."

"At least there's still hope that Jamison could pull through."

This had the effect of brightening Miloje's countenance. "Oh, yes? Well, that really would be the culmination of all of our hopes. Perhaps he *will* revive with the answer to the riddles. Or at least enough insight that he and Art Mallard can finish what they began."

Blackforest made a face, scratching behind his beard. "I'll admit: I don't like trusting the future of this department to such weird people."

"Nor do I," Miloje said with a wily grin. "But we must accept such hope as we can."

"Our situation really is that desperate," Blackforest agreed, sans any amusement. "Every day this goes unresolved is one day closer to the next Harbor bombing."

Presently, there was a knock at the door. Reaching silent consensus with Miloje, Blackforest turned to open it. "Yes?"

"Pardon me, Sir," a very crestfallen cadet said, holding his bobby in his hands. "I have some news. I'm not entirely sure how to break it. There's... a delegation here from another police department. They need to see you immediately, Sir."

Blackforest deferred to Miloje, who with his silence conveyed he knew nothing about this. Turning back to the cadet, the DA asked the operative question... whether or not he knew it at the time. "Which department are they from?"

Chapter 12

"Deborah's been gone a long time, hasn't she?" Adam asked rather sheepishly.

Horus blinked. "Hm?" The question corralled him back to a reality he didn't remember wandering away from. "Yes, I suppose she has."

"...Think that means trouble?"

"It may mean something's come up," Horus admitted. "I'm not at all sure."

Adam's sense of anxiety suddenly shifted its focus. "Horus – what's the matter? You haven't been yourself all day. Don't tell me it's just the Whiffle thing." His exposed eye made a quick probe of Horus' cast. "Is it about... whatever happened with your arm?"

Horus let out a slow breath. He'd always hated conversations like this – the tedium of telling people he was fine, and none of them ever listening. But abruptly, it occurred to him that he must've heard – whether once, twice, or several times – that it actually helps to talk openly about what ails you every now and again. Perhaps this was an ideal time to try it out... in relatively anonymous confidence. And after all, Adam was a client, and clients were obliged to be very open about *their* problems, if they had any good sense. Maybe it was only fair to be open in return...

"Alright," Horus answered, looking down at his own arm. "I admit: It was a harrowing morning in the worst kind of way."

"...What happened?"

Horus shrugged. "It was a dragon attack."

Adam seemed to mull this over for a bit. "Wow. I can't imagine."

"You really never can, until you find yourself in the gauntlet," Horus explained, shifting in his chair. "That was the first lesson I learned. You hear about these kinds of things, and it pricks your sympathy. But then you see it with your own eyes, and you just can't make sense of it. Everyone there was merely going about their daily business. They didn't even try to get in the dragon's way. No, but then again, I suppose a few of the bravest ones made a stand. I don't imagine their courage was any better rewarded than the unassuming way we all wound up..." He stopped, as words simply seemed to fail him. "It was... a great injustice. And it's left me feeling very perplexed."

"It really is a shame," Adam sympathized. "We try to live our lives equitably, and what do we get? My eye. Your arm. No matter what we do – no matter how we toe the line – it could all go wrong in a heartbeat."

"Well, of course, we have other reasons to conduct ourselves admirably besides our own personal welfare. We're social creatures, as we were designed to be. We have each other to look out for. We have the greater good."

"And the mandates of the state to go with it," Adam chuckled. "Life's mostly a lot of doing what they tell us to because they told us. But the whole 'law and order' bit... it's kind of a thin façade sometimes, isn't it? They act like they run the show, but can they argue with a dragon? They haven't even been able to keep a guy back from jaywalking."

"Well, the shortcomings of the state can be rather glaring at times," Horus admitted. "But ultimately, it's what the state is meant to stand for that's more important. It gives us clear and present incentive to live by rules and virtues – two things we absolutely need. Because without them, we're no different than the dragon." He grinned, feeling that his own impromptu lecture had reminded him of the basics he'd spent the last several hours in a fog without. "I find myself in your debt, Adam," he said. "You've already helped me more than you know."

Adam shrugged, making a bit of a funny face. "I can't see how I've helped at all, but you're welcome," he scoffed.

Horus leaned back, scratching thoughtfully behind one ear. "Now, what were we talking about before? Deborah's long absence. She was going to find out what – if anything – the prosecution means to do now that Whiffle has impeached himself."

"A strangely fruity word, that – *impeached*," Gord mused aloud. All of a sudden, he turned from his window. "Horus, I've been thinking."

Only now made aware of Gord's presence, Horus nonetheless nodded at him. "Naturally."

"I mean, about your case."

"Oh," Horus said, taken aback. "Well, that *is* unexpected."

"You say you impeached Whiffle Caruthers, but you never did get him to confess to his perjury, did you?"

Horus frowned. "No. Tragically, I never did."

"Well, what if he doubles down on his story one last time?" Gord asked.

The question had Horus at a loss. "You'll forgive me, but I don't see how he could do that."

Gord held out his hands as if to illustrate. "We've established that Whiffle and Adam have a history of bad blood. That they've known each other for years. You also happened to learn that the jaywalking-shoe was in Whiffle's size. And of course, there's the little matter of the stick – Whiffle's own polearm."

"Yes, and yes," Horus said. "What is all this supposed to add up to?"

"Another frameup," Gord answered. "The reverse of the frameup we wanted to prove, you might say."

"Meaning what? That *Adam* was trying to frame *Whiffle*?"

Gord nodded. "Exactly. Whiffle could make it out that Adam used a shoe in *his* size and stole *his* polearm to pin the crime on *him*. In that case, he still could've witnessed Adam stashing it, just as he said he did."

Horus took a moment to run the numbers, forward and back. He could hardly believe it. Gord was right. "That's... insidious... but it *does* fit. With a story like that, Whiffle could point the finger back at Adam and avoid the charge of perjury he never admitted to, all at the same time."

"You're close, but just left of the mark," Deborah's voice interjected. They turned to find her leaning against the doorframe with her arms crossed. "I'm sure that's just the narrative Whiffle would've *liked* to push, if he could've got away with it. But I'm afraid he's constrained to admit to one major fib. He never did see Adam stash the shoe on a stick. He played a very different part that night."

Horus and Adam exchanged a look, before returning their questioning eyes to her. "What part is that?" Horus asked.

"He was 'the Caller' we've been wondering about," Deborah revealed. "The one who drew Sergeant Basil's attention in the first place – directed him which way the jaywalker went."

"How in the world did this come to light?" Horus ventured, growing more and more bewildered by it all.

"Basil came forward about it. He said that during testimony, Whiffle struck him as oddly familiar. But when he suddenly started *shouting*, he confirmed Basil's suspicions. The way he carried on about Adam 'getting away' struck all the same notes the Sergeant remembered from the night of the crime."

Horus shook his head. "Well, there. That *proves* Whiffle perjured himself. Why then should we entertain this modified narrative of his?"

Deborah turned up a palm. "He claims he altered his story to protect himself. He says he had knowledge of the items used in the crime because they were stolen from him, but he didn't want it known that they were his, since that could've painted him as a suspect himself. He was also trying to avoid admitting he knew Adam so that his testimony didn't appear biased."

"Alright. So he had *reasons* for lying. The fact remains he *lied*. Can we responsibly proceed under the assumption he's telling the full truth this time? The court shouldn't uphold anything he has to say."

"You don't have to convince *me*, Boss," Deborah replied. "If it weren't for Sergeant Basil's revelation, I'd say they were at the end of their rope. But he *is* a reliable witness... and he places Whiffle right back in the center of the whole thing. All the prosecution can do is try to reconcile the facts. And unfortunately, Whiffle's new story does that."

Horus sighed, resting his head against his hand. "We've let this case devolve into hearsay and name-calling."

"But that's good in a way, isn't it?" Adam piped up. "It's my word against his. He says I used the stick to frame him, I say he used it to frame me. The difference is, we already know he lied."

"But *we're* still up against the astronomical odds," Horus reminded him. "The odds against you being bowled over by the real Lazarus. I'd be hopeless to explain how something like that played so perfectly into Whiffle's hand. What we should've had was a mistrial for lack of credible testimony. But as long as the case is still on, they have the plausible story of a known liar against the implausible story of a man who's come under suspicion once before. That's far from the clear-cut thing I'd like it to be." He looked back over at Gord – his unlikely benefactor from a minute ago. "What do you think, Gord? Apparently, you've got a knack for this. Any ideas how to proceed?"

Gord turned to regard him, looking a tad befuddled. "Sorry. I'm afraid I wandered back into postulating the marketability of armpit removal surgery. What was the question?"

"Well, never mind," Horus fairly groaned. "Far be it from me to interrupt such grand machinations with our little problems. But this does put us in a pickle."

"Well, I'm only sorry to bring such bad news..." Deborah proffered, "... and to be so long in bringing it. It's no excuse, but the department's a madhouse right now."

Horus' ears perked back up. "Something more than we already knew about?"

She got a shell-shocked look on her face, just then. "If you'll believe it, yes. But I'm afraid it'll have to wait."

She followed her comment with just the sort of nod that made Horus realize he'd overlooked something. The moment he checked his watch, he knew what. "I really have let time get away from me. There's a paint can across town with my name on it."

"You going to be alright with just the one arm, Boss?" Deborah asked as he leapt into action.

"There's no choice but to make do," he replied dismissively. "I should be fine with a brush."

* * *

"I daresay you've made marked improvement since you began this undertaking, Mr. Templar," Doctor Forasius cheered Horus on, just as he managed yet another trip back and forth to the bucket without so much as a single dribble of paint.

"That's kind of you to say, Forasius," Horus replied. He donned a sarcastic grin. "But then, I'm not sure I could've gotten much worse."

Forasius chuckled. "Perhaps not." He made a quick scan of the immediate area. "Have you a second brush, Sir? I've time and a foot to spare."

"Are you sure? I do begin to feel bad accepting so much help. I hope you haven't counted me out just because I'm down one little arm."

"Not at all," Forasius said, nevertheless taking a second brush he found leaning against the can. "Although – and I hope you'll forgive my saying so – I rather suspect it was your dominant arm that's been damaged."

"I shouldn't be surprised you noticed," Horus replied, brushing first up, then down. "Did you simply take note of which hand I was using before? Or has my work not actually improved as much as you claimed?"

"Principally, the strokes on the wall don't look the same," Forasius explained. "You may be interested to know this is something I've been studying – the imperfect symmetry of the body. It started out as a journal piece on the rare hox gene mutation of localized translational symmetry, but it has since broadened out to include the full spectrum of minor, perfectly mundane bilateral incongruencies. The very fact of the dominant hand phenomenon is a perfect example. But even in the uncommon case of the ambidextrous fellow, he would never be able to – for instance – sign his name in quite the same way with both hands. Why, even fingerprints are not perfect mirror images from one hand to the other."

"That *is* interesting," Horus mused. "I never really stopped to think about it. But none of us are perfectly symmetrical from left to right, are we?"

"Oh, there are *some* instances in nature – don't get me wrong," Forasius said, finally joining Horus at the wall with his own brush. "Queen Meduselda exhibit it in their crystalline features. Phage are walking incarnations of mathematical precision. You would have to break one open to find anything with less than perfect radial symmetry on those chaps."

"Well, I hope your paper turns out," said Horus. "Sounds like it gets into things well beyond my understanding. But then, I've no idea what it takes to impress *your* colleagues. Something tells me they're a tough crowd."

"They are. But I daresay I do well enough for myself." Forasius turned his mask to face Horus. "What of your endeavors, Sir? In all this time we haven't so much discussed them. Is it really true your client is supposed to have been a serial jaywalker?"

"*Supposed* to have been, yes."

Forasius shuddered. "A terrible thing."

"It is. And made all the more terrible because once again, the State wants its conviction more than it wants justice. I proved their witness furnished the evidence in the crime himself, and all he has to do is change his story to say Adam first robbed him and then committed his heinous acts. Now I'll have to prove he's lying again. I *shouldn't* have to, but I do. And the greatest trouble is, I don't know how yet."

"The witness claims he was robbed of his shoe?"

"Not *just* his shoe," Horus explained. "More critically, the polearm the shoe was attached to."

Forasius paused between paint strokes. "What's this, now? The shoe was not simply *worn* in the crime?"

Horus shook his head. "It *couldn't* be. Certainly not by my client. It was much too small for him."

The Doctor appeared more and more intensely interested. "But isn't this jaywalking fellow well-known for leaving a print behind to exhibit his misdeeds?"

"Yes," Horus answered – puzzled by Forasius' line of questioning.

"But surely it's a muddled thing, then? Hardly recognizable as a shoe print?"

"No. By all accounts, the prints are quite full and detailed."

Forasius paused in apparent disbelief. “My good man, I must apologize I haven’t wandered into this subject much earlier. I see now that I had what you needed all along.”

Horus’ ears perked. “What do you mean?”

“Well, it’s extraordinary, but this is all quite tied-in with the bit I was just telling you!” Forasius burst. “Just as the left hand cannot perfectly imitate the right, one can’t simply put a shoe on the end of a pole and expect to leave the same print as he would with a proper foot! Certainly not a *Human* foot, where all the business is at the fore, and they walk heel-to-toe.” He tried to pantomime the Human stride – demonstrating something of his own point in the laughable way it looked nothing like their locomotion. But in the process, he absently kicked the paint can over. “Oh, Creators save me! What a blunder! And you were so careful to keep the paint off the floor this time, too. My dear Nokkaeru will be rather unimpressed with me now. She oft remarks how excitable I am.”

“The floor needed to be redone from my past visits anyway,” Horus tried to encourage him. “We’ll make it right. But now, you *have* to finish your thought! You’re *sure* the shoe-on-a-stick couldn’t leave a convincing print on the ground?”

Forasius regarded his mess thoughtfully. “We’ve Human neighbors down the street, and surely some manner of stick or other hereabouts. I can *tell* you with confidence it wouldn’t work, Mr. Templar. But far better to *show* you, yes?”

* * *

STOMP

STOMP

STOMP-STOMP

“There, you see?” Forasius asked exuberantly. “No matter how we secure the thing, we can’t simulate the rolling pressure of a foot!”

Once again, Horus admired his own handiwork, finding that much as before, he couldn’t get a good, full print off the front of the shoe. The paint left behind on the floor was concentrated at the inner side of the heel, with only a bit of the front sole making any other mark. “Well, I’ll be,” Horus marveled. “Still… perhaps with a bit more technique…”

“Go on trying, then!” Forasius invited him. “You’ll only have to admit it’s useless!”

Horus hobbled as if with a crutch, leaving a whole trail of prints. "I'm trying to roll through the 'step', now," he narrated. "I wonder what difference it would make if I could use my better arm."

"Not difference enough! Nor has your added finesse! The prints are still quite pitiful."

Horus came back around and leaned against the broom handle, scrutinizing each of the many prints left all over. Just as Forasius claimed, none of them really held up to the few rows they'd convinced Nokkaeru's much-bewildered neighbor to make with his foot still in the shoe. Horus smiled, nodding his approval. Much as he still loathed to bring Whiffle's many falsehoods down on him, the truth had to come out... and this spelled the final resolution of the matter. It was a victory. It was a welcome ray of hope.

And then, the front door began to open.

Horus and Forasius stood frozen in place, watching Nokkaeru's long neck crane this way, and that. Silent, breathless suspense gripped their hearts.

"What in the blazes...!!?!!"

Chapter 13

Prepared as he was for the morning, it was to come much earlier than Horus expected. He bolted upright from his bed in a cold pant, eyes darting all around to meet what had spooked him. But the longer he searched, and the pain in his arm calmed its throbbing, the more he began to reconstruct things. The sound he'd awakened to hadn't come from without, but within. He'd been dreaming. Reliving the attack. Presently, he remembered the final moment of the dream – the culminating horror that shook him from his slumber. It wasn't when he was struck by the tail. It wasn't the near-miss as the creature's bulk passed right over him. It wasn't even the blazing heat on his back as he made his final retreat. It was no pain or anxiety of his own at all. Truly, it was the *last* thing that should've distressed him. It was the sound of the dragon's death knell.

Just as he realized this, a haunting echo of the cry replayed, and Horus felt a great emptiness in his chest. He about cursed himself. Why, of all things, should the dragon's pain cause him grief? It only got what it had coming to it – what it surely earned many times over in the space of that morning alone. How warped was he, to feel any sympathy for a monster like that?

* * *

After only a few minutes' restlessness, Horus resolved to take a pre-dawn walk and clear his head. He had to push past the unwanted thought that an early start was the prelude to his troubles the day before. Moving quickly on from that, he next realized he had no place in mind to go. A brief roundup of old, familiar locations reminded him that he hadn't seen his own office in what seemed like forever. There was no question it was high time to check on it.

As a warm sun began to appear and the Phantom Light cast its long morning shadows, Horus found his timing was indeed on the nose. Not so much because he had any hope of finding the office among the literally endless string of cars, but rather because he chanced to be in just the right place to catch an informative bit of eavesdropping in his keen ears.

"You've got to be kidding!" a very exasperated engineer exclaimed. "After everything we went through just to get all this hooked up?!"

"Oh, come on! You can't seriously want to go on running it like this," the message-runner scoffed. "I'm telling you the Comptroller's policies are getting the kybosh, and you're complaining? Don't you understand? Things are going back to normal!"

"Yeah, well, try being the guy that has to *put* things back to normal!"

The argument went on and on from there, but Horus got the message loud and clear. Another funky chapter of St. Argonsburg's illustrious saga was coming to a close.

And this was not to be the morning's only revelation. As per usual, once he was tuned-in to the chatter on the streets, he could hardly tune back out...

"Hey, crazy about that jaywalker, huh? Who'd've thought they'd actually catch up with him?"

"How do you figure? Sounds like they botched the case again. I tell ya, they never make the charges stick anymore in this town."

"You mean, it's already gone to trial? Boy, what else did I miss?"

...Another block, another bite of gossip...

"I can't believe it. I'm going to lose my second job? How am I ever going to provide for my family?"

"The same way you did before, dummy."

...And then, a bigger one...

"I'm telling you, they shot him down in the street!"

"*No*. The PI they got to find their spy for them? Why wasn't it in the paper?"

"You got me, Pal."

"But *why* would they shoot him? What reason could they have?"

"That's what *I'm* saying! Nothing makes sense anymore."

...This gave Horus pause. He'd learned about Detective Jamison's shooting from Deborah at the tail end of the night before, and it had certainly been disturbing enough then. To further learn that the whole incident was being hushed got his dander up all over again.

But before he could long brood on it, the next little snippet he overheard did the natural Human thing and synthesized the entire roundup of everything wrong in St. Argonsburg into one massive, fully-integrated dread...

"A fellow's got to wonder what's next. They didn't get the alarm up until twenty minutes after the dragon landed. They closed the mole investigation and half the people who worked on it end up dead. They stir up the entire city with all these hipshot innovations and change their minds overnight. They got Lazarus, and his shoe to boot, and yet they're about a step away from letting him skate. And that's just in the last week."

"You ever wonder if... maybe... old Lazarus is the smart one? I mean, what if the rest of us are just kidding ourselves at this point? What if..." and this was the hint that crowned them all, "...what if the Czarina doesn't really have a handle on things anymore?"

...Though his friend was very quick and harsh to correct him, Horus couldn't unhear the last man's suggestion. Had it really come to that? Were the people becoming so doubtful of their leadership that they would dare to speak of it aloud? Granted, Horus himself was more than professionally acquainted with a number of the Czarina's foibles. He knew very well that in some important respects, she was only a person herself. But he'd never dreamed to question the *legitimacy* of her office – only the wisdom in the ways she chose to exact her sovereign indignation from time to time. The court system served as the necessary moderator of her whims, and though there were certainly a few laws in the nation of Jast-Madiir that fell short of equity and ought to be changed, Horus' confidence in the administration had never truly been shaken. He never thought he'd see the day when there was this much disconnect between the Czarina and the common folk. And he was sure all the attempts being made to keep some of these matters quiet had only exasperated the problem. People were finding out what was being kept back from them... and worse: they were finding it out with many of the details heightened.

Now of course, he had no influence over most of the peoples' concerns. But even over the one he did, all he could do was lament more than ever the prevalence of the 'guilty until proven guilty' mentality. All he could do was wish all the more that proving innocence in court and proving innocence in the eyes of the masses could simply be one and the same. He hated to contribute to everyone's alarm. He hated to lend to the sense that the system was failing them. But what else could he do? His duty was to his client. Consequences be darned, he had to represent Adam to the best of his ability. And in all this, his one great consolation was his certainty that his client *was* innocent. Despite all the odds and uncertainties that had come and gone since, the truth – it turned out – had been as plain as Adam's great big foot from the start. He couldn't have done it. It wasn't possible. Horus knew that. And soon the court would, too. That would just have to be good enough. There simply wasn't any satisfying the people once they made up their minds to brood about things. As further exemplified when Horus rounded the next street corner. He rolled his eyes at the sight of the latest bit of drama...

Across the street, the Onyxadon-sign-guy was exhibiting his newly customized bulletin:

"Onyxadon – already here?"

* * *

CLACK

"Court is now in session," Judge Thutmose announced into the unnecessarily dark and disconsolate room. "We will commence with a report from the prosecution, detailing certain developments which have arisen in light of the prescribed interrogation of the previous witness."

Previous witness, Horus thought, noting the careful absence of such adjectives as 'impeached' or 'perjured' in Thutmose's phrasing. "If the court please," Horus called out as he stood. "I feel it is my duty to remind your Honor that the witness in question was bound away for his interrogation on charges of perjury. Interrogation or no, the introduction of new testimony from a source that has already proven himself inherently unreliable is unconscionable. It is therefore that I motion for a mistrial."

Thutmose shook his head. "Your motion is rejected, Counselor. It is enough that we proceed with due caution. We will admit the findings of the interrogation inasmuch as we can confirm them against the facts and corroborating testimony." He clacked his gavel again.

"Well, *alright,*" Horus said as if to shrug, and sat back down.

The judge squinted at him. Evidently, he didn't much appreciate an ominous 'Well, alright,' in his court. On the other hand, Horus soon learned that Adam wasn't altogether fond of this, either.

"Hey," he whispered. "That's it? You're just going to let them go ahead? I mean... I guess I thought you'd push a little harder."

"Not to worry, Adam," Horus quietly assured him. "Everything they're about to introduce will be moot as soon as I can present your defense."

A smile slowly crept across Adam's face. "Moot, huh?"

"Yes," Horus guaranteed. "Absolutely irrelevant."

Adam nodded. "Well, okay then. That's what I like to hear."

"I thought you might."

By this time, Blucille was facing the gallery from in front of the witness stand, looking very focused at a stack of papers in her hand. "I will now introduce this sworn statement made by Whiffle Caruthers. It is the corpus of the court-ordered interrogation."

Purely for sake of good form, Horus stood. "Objection. Entertaining the notion that Caruthers can offer us anything meaningful, he should've been recalled, rather than resorting to this adif... adif..." *Drat*. Even with recent elocution exercises, he couldn't say the word at need. And now, everyone was giving him a funny look. "...To this sworn statement. It's not best evidence."

"Objection overruled," Thutmose ordered tiredly. "I have – in effect – already granted this affidavit to be admitted. The man Caruthers demonstrated criminal contempt of court the last time he was brought to the stand, and so *will not* be called again."

Horus shrugged it off. "Suit yourself." He fetched another distinct frown from the judge.

"Proceed, Ms. Cordon."

* * *

For many pages of deposition and a lengthy second examination of Sergeant Basil, Horus permitted Blucille the floor without further outburst. Though Blucille hadn't given him the evil eye early on, as Judge Thutmose had, he could tell that his silence since then was unnerving her. No interjections to belabor the many inconsistencies between Whiffle's original testimony and his affidavit. No chances taken to cast doubt on the certainty of Basil's late-in-coming identification of Whiffle as 'The Caller'. Horus elected to forfeit his cross-examination. Yes, he could tell *that* in particular had her worried. It sent a clear message that he regarded Whiffle's new role in the night of the crime as either irrelevant, or worse – a turn that actually played right into his hand. Her eyes on him when the words 'no questions' left his mouth might as well have been grapefruits.

"If there is nothing more for the prosecution to present, we will begin with the defense tomorrow at eight o'clock," Thutmose said.

Blucille stood. She hesitated before saying, "The prosecution rests, your Honor."

"Very well. Court is adjourned." With a last tap of his sound block, they all began to disperse. Blucille was not slow in coming over to Horus' table...

"What exactly have you got up your sleeve, Horus?" she asked outright. "It must be something big."

"It is," he replied, feeling not at all smug. He was enjoying the chance to make his long-time rival sweat less and less all the time. "The smart money says a liar always doubles down. I'm afraid yours has."

She alternated a look between Horus and Adam. "I don't understand how Whiffle could hate anyone as much as your client – *insist* on his guilt so passionately – unless it was true."

"Unfortunately, we don't have to understand," Horus countered. "Adam simply can't have done it the way Whiffle claims he did. Nor any other way."

Blucille wasn't satisfied, but there was nothing left to say. She simply left. Horus turned back to his client, finding that he alone in the sea of faces was cheerful. Horus wished he could share his cheer. He was serving truth, and justice... even if no one besides himself and Adam could see that. If there was anyone who should've been used to a feeling like that, it was Horus. Why, then, did he still feel so rotten?

* * *

Any time Blucille refrained from picking at her food for too long a time, Art was there to pick at his. Another disinterested little probe of a morsel with his fork and he'd done his part. A few long seconds later, Blucille mirrored the action, keeping dinner well on course to be eaten approximately never.

"Guess things didn't go so hot in court taday, huh?" he reluctantly ventured.

"No, I don't think so," she answered – eyes low, until with some effort she raised them. "How is Detective Jamison?"

"No change," Art replied. "At least he's still hangin' in there."

From there, the picking resumed.

But finally, Art raised one ear, and then the other. He set his fork down. "What're we doin' here?" he asked. "Every time we get a good grip on that 'We'll make it work somehow' attitude, we lose it again. Why do we keep doing that, Blucille? Huh? Why do we keep forgetting everything we've already beat, just ta be here?"

He got a little grin out of her. It was a start. "I don't know, Art. I guess we're just natural worriers."

He shook his head. "Uh-uh. Not me. I'm hardboiled by trade, and I'm a little shook up from this morning, but I'm no worrier." He took his fork back up and hurriedly forced a bite. "Mm. This stuff's really good once ya make up your mind ta eat it."

"I'm sure it is," she chuckled nervously. "I'm afraid I'm just not all that hungry."

"Well, c'mon, then," he said, standing up from the candlelit table. "How 'bout a spot of dancing? You wouldn't turn that down, would ya?"

She smiled a bit more. "Oh, what the Heck?" Replacing her napkin to the board, she joined him on her feet. "We *did* just do the impossible today, didn't we? We got my folks' permission! We'd have to be crazy not to celebrate *that*!"

"Darn tootin'!" he agreed, taking her hand and leading her out onto the open floor of his home.

The two of them danced only a handful of steps together before Blucille laughed self-consciously. "This is nice... but a little awkward without any music."

"Well, now... I'll just have ta fix that..." Art boded winsomely. He cleared his throat. "*Daa-da, da-de-dah, da-dah...*"

That really got her laughing, and she whapped him. "Okay, never mind! I'm sure we can do better without *that*, thank you."

"Whatever ya like, Darlin'."

They went on to dance with a bit more coordination. Blucille rested her head against his chest. But just when things began to feel nice and cozy, she sighed. "At the risk of killing the mood all over again... you mentioned my parents had some stipulations. Dare I ask what they were?"

He shrugged. "Nothing too crazy. They just wanted us to nitpick and hassle each other half ta death."

She looked up at him with dreamy eyes. "Is that all? Well, I'm sure we can manage that much."

He nodded. "For a little while, anyway."

They returned to their cozy twirling. It wasn't so very long before Blucille sighed again – a more contented sigh this time. "You know, this is just what I needed all along."

"What? *This*?" Art chuckled. "A clumsy little dance?"

"It's not just the dance, Art," she explained. "I needed someone to show me it's okay to see the bright side of things. To teach me not to let every trouble drag me that much farther down. The bad times come... but they go, too. I don't have to hold on to them forever. I was only torturing myself."

That put Art right on the verge of getting misty. He never realized he did all that. "Glad I could help, Silly Snout." With a little false bravado, he tried to leave it at that. But after a while, the big lug in him couldn't help returning the compliment. "Ya know: I really needed you, too."

She met his eyes with hers. "Really?"

He nodded. "Yup."

She shook her head – scoffed. "What would you need a girl like me for?"

This question demanded a moment of thought. Fortunately, a most profound answer presented itself soon enough. "I dunno. I just did."

She smiled, resting her head yet again.

They twirled.

They held each other close.

...And then, there was a knock at the door.

Art could hear her grimace.

"We better get that," he said.

"It's going to be work," she intoned.

"I know. We better get it anyway."

They reluctantly parted. Art stepped up to his door and opened it. Sure enough: In the soft, low light, they found a couple of policemen on the porch. Art didn't recognize either one of them. "Hello?" he asked, unsure.

"Private Smithers, Sir – seeking Blucille Cordon," the frontmost policeman replied. "We were told we would find her here."

"I'm right here, uh, Smithers?" Blucille said from behind Art, sounding quite unsure herself. "What's the situation?"

"Rather urgent I'm afraid, Ma'am," the private said. "We're here to inform you of a change in your employment."

She blinked her utter confusion. It was well known that people all over the city were receiving termination notices for their second and third jobs. But that hardly applied in her case. "Why, there must be some mistake. I was never even conscripted to a second job."

Smithers shook his head. "No mistake, Ms. Cordon. I'm not sure of any extraneous jobs, but yours has changed rather suddenly." He solemnly removed his bobby, and the police standing further from the threshold along with him. "You see – most regrettably – the District Attorney of Cape Deltrix has passed. As per the conditions of your tutelage under Hamilton

Blackforest, you've been promoted to his office forthwith. We're going to have to ask you to come back with us to the Cape at once."

Art didn't remember breathing – didn't remember blinking. Above all, he couldn't remember Blucille turning to him and wearing that heart-stopping look of disbelieving devastation. It was as if he'd lapsed from time and space, and quite without any thought, returned, feeling more displaced and confused than he'd ever known he could feel. He understood the words that Smithers said. But *how* could he have said them? Art failed utterly to comprehend...

"Ma'am, I do apologize, but we really must be off."

Whatever the policeman's appeals, Art found Blucille was still looking helplessly at him. "Art... what...? How do we...?"

"We will," he said, not even knowing where it came from. "We'll find a way."

"Ma'am, please," Smithers insisted.

She turned to the private, looking at him up and down with eyes of dread. She turned back to Art, who could only urge her on by that same mysterious reflex. "Go ahead. It's going to be alright, Blucille. I promise. We'll find a way."

She took her first step... and her second. She slowly passed into shadow as her feet crossed the threshold. Art watched as her eyes caught the candlelight when she turned one last time in the dark, before the other policeman closed the door. He was left standing there – alone – with only the broken sound of his own voice.

"We'll find a way..."

Chapter 14

News of Blucille's sudden departure reached Horus at the speed of Deborah, and he carried that momentum with him right up to the DA's office, much to the fright of anyone in the SAPD who had the misfortune of nearly stepping in his way.

"Mr. Templar!" one of the secretaries called after him. She quite valiantly even tried to put herself between him and Hamilton's door. "I'm afraid Mr. Blackforest is..."

"He'll see me now," Horus explained, walking right by her.

SLAM

He had the instant attention of Blackforest himself, a number of ADAs, and even a few judges who'd congregated around his desk. Blackforest resorted at once to a tired expression. "Oh, good. A concerned citizen here to voice his criticism. What perfect timing. Something in particular I can help you with, Horus?"

"You know why I'm here," Horus stated. "You have to get her back."

There was a flash of remorse in Blackforest's eyes, before he quickly looked back down at whatever documents they'd all been strategizing over. "What a boon you've come by to share that idea. I surely never would've thought of it myself. Now if you'll kindly excuse us..."

"Hamilton, for once in your cowardly existence, you're going to have to push back on something," Horus pressed him. "You're going to demand her back, and you're not going to take no for an answer."

"Yes, because any problem can be solved if you're just bold and brash enough," Blackforest scoffed rather absently. "You really think everything in the world is that simple? Try walking a mile in my shoes, Horus. You should be so unlucky."

"You just don't want to try. You're doing what you always do and hiding behind the idea that it's out of your hands. But choosing not to act is still a choice. Can't you see how much your decision is hurting people?"

Finally, Blackforest threw an open hand on the desk and pushed himself up straight, eyes ablaze. "I'm the District Attorney of St. Argonsburg. *Every* decision I make hurts people."

Horus had no answer for this, except to enter a pitted stare-down. For long seconds, neither he nor Blackforest flinched.

"...Should we go?" an ADA meekly inquired.

Blackforest nodded in his general direction. "Yes, please do. I promise this won't take long."

Everyone else slowly cleared out, leaving Blackforest and Horus still deadlocked. Even after the door was shut, there was no quick end to the silence. But at last, Blackforest was the first to speak.

"So, somehow you've got it in your head that I was just going to let a thing like this go without a peep. Your sterling vote of confidence is always appreciated. I regret to inform you that reality played out somewhat differently. You see, I've already met with the Chairman of Jurisdictional Human Resources Management. I tried to explain to him that Blucille still required significant training before she'd be ready to take over as a full District Attorney. He disagreed – citing my own reports of her progress over the years. From there, I had to be more upfront. I did everything I could to convince him that she'd become an indispensable asset of the SAPD, and that something else would have to be worked out to fill the void in Cape Deltrix. I tried to lobby for her as my *own* successor. He reminded me that her transfer had been the point and purpose of her training from the beginning. He was also quick to let me know that if I'd become unduly reliant on her, it was my own fault, and I'd have to remedy it myself. But I didn't even stop there. I implored him to at least transfer a one Private Investigator Artimus Mallard along with her. I made my appeal to the fact that they were engaged, and that the separation would cause her undue strain during an already challenging transition. But he couldn't be interested in personalities. Cape Deltrix – he said – had no need of additional Private Investigators. Not like St. Argonsburg, where he was aware that a prominent Detective had recently been shot, and had a very poor prognosis." Blackforest paused, folding his arms. "So you tell me, Horus: What did I hold back? Or what stroke of cleverness did I fail to dream up that would've worked all this out? You come up with a good answer to that and get back with me. I'll be only too happy to hear it. In the meantime, I've got a lot on my plate." He reached for and retrieved a fistful of papers from his desk. "There've been hundreds of cases of people failing to report to work on time in the last few days – falling asleep on the job – coming up well short of their quotas. I've been in nearly constant contact with the Czarina's office, and it's all I could do for these people to get most of their terminations of employment retroactively changed to an earlier date, so the charges no longer apply. She didn't want to show *any* leniency, at first. I had to convince her to shift the balance of the blame to the other object of her wrath – Royal Comptroller

Thangorodrim himself. Yes… *I* had to ransom these people at another man's expense. I have to live with that. I have to carry it out myself. And I have to do it all with my right hand suddenly cut off. So, go ahead. Blame all this on me, if it makes you feel any better. I can take it."

Outwardly, Horus didn't seem much moved. He kept his stern face on until he was satisfied that everything possible had already been done, and there was nothing more he could say. Grudgingly, he started for the door. But about the time he got there, he decided there was something that ought to be said. "Hamilton: I'm sorry."

"Obviously," Blackforest growled. "And so am I." He shook his head – ears folded back – reaching for his pipe. "It's not like your criticism was completely unfounded. I know I've ducked a few stands I should've taken in the past. What can I say? The office takes a toll. Sometimes, there's a terrible cost to make things come out right. Sometimes they don't come out right no matter what you do."

* * *

As the night wore on, Horus came shuffling back to the Ecre Point warehouse, finding it poetically empty. He sat himself dejectedly at the piano, resting his head on his hand and looking down at the keys, finding no inspiration to play anything either distractingly happy or sympathetically sad – even if he had the use of both arms to do so. He thought about going out to find either Deborah, or Art himself – little though he knew how he might console either one. Morose as he was, it still seemed as if there was a deeper sense of misery he *ought* to feel, but was presently locked out of. That all he might come up with to say if he had Art standing right in front of him this very moment was how inconsequential the hopes and designs of the heart are in the vast scheme of things. It was a sobering motif that had plagued him since the dragon. But to see it echoed in Art's life so shortly thereafter put things well past sobriety. He felt… numb. He felt hollow.

Presently, his ear swiveled to meet something stirring in the back room. Apparently, the place was not as empty as it seemed. He engaged his olfactory powers at once in the mystery. *Adam…*

Horus stood from the bench, ambling for the next room. Sure enough, when he got there, he found Adam – breaking out some gauze and bandaging.

"Oh. Hello, Horus," Adam said. "Didn't hear you come in. Actually, I began to think I wouldn't see anyone till tomorrow. It's getting pretty late."

"That it is," Horus agreed a bit dubiously. "I'm sorry if I've kept you waiting for me."

Adam shrugged. "Not really."

Horus blinked. "Well, then – not meaning to be rude – might I ask what you *are* still doing here at this hour?"

"Changing the bandage on my eye, at the moment," Adam laughed. Horus watched him in profile as he exposed the medical tape. "I have to warn you," he intoned, "the eye's still quite a mess. You might want to step back out for a minute if you've got a weak stomach."

"I doubt my constitution would fail me now." He couldn't help that he still felt confused about Adam's presence. "You'll forgive me, but isn't that something you could do just as well at home?"

"I suppose I *could*," he chortled. "But you know, I really like this place. It's classy. I got to thinking this whole thing's going to be over pretty soon, and I'd miss being around. Figured I might as well enjoy it while I could." He turned his head long enough to look at Horus for a moment. He hadn't yet removed the old bandage. "I would've asked permission, of course, but no one's been around."

Horus cleared his throat. "Yes, well... something came up."

He glanced at Horus a second time, a nervous look on his face. "Something *else*?"

"Nothing you should be concerned about," Horus was quick to assure him. "It's not about the case. It's a personal matter."

"Well, apparently I helped you with one of those before," Adam reminded him as he fished out a few squares of gauze. "Why don't you tell me about it?"

Horus dithered. "It's... well... not as much a personal problem of *mine*, as it is Art's. His fiancé – you'll undoubtedly remember Blucille Cordon – was quite abruptly transferred to a new office in Cape Deltrix this evening."

"What a shame..." The patch came away from Adam's eye, though from Horus' vantage point the bridge of his nose concealed the allegedly gruesome damage. "He must be devastated."

"I can only imagine. I haven't seen him since I got the news." His eyes fell. Simply speaking of the matter seemed to bring forth some of his suppressed emotion. "Really, we're all devastated. Art's a good friend. The love he and Ms. Cordon shared was... a picture of mutual reliance. It was nothing short of transformative. If I'm... quite honest... I don't know how they'll get along without each other now."

"Well, then... maybe they shouldn't."

Horus' ears snapped fully upright. The cryptically simple suggestion – not to mention the patronizing amusement Adam offered it with – prickled him. "What do you mean?"

"It's really very simple, Horus," he explained. "If there's something you want out of life, you just reach out and *take* it. I mean, after all, why not? Just because a few upstarts try to force a bunch of rules down your throat? They can't back it up half as good as you think. If you're quick, and clever, they'll never stop you in time. The best they can hope is for you to slip up." He turned his head, revealing a more heinously bruised, bloodshot eye than anything Horus dreamed could be concealed under a mere bandage, and a smile to match. "Because once you make up your mind to color outside the lines, there's nothing left to hold you back."

Horus couldn't believe it. "You... you're..."

"What? *Lazarus*?" Adam mocked him. "As if there was ever a chance it was anyone else. Oh, but it's been a *ball*, Horus – this whole charade. And I have you alone to thank for it. You see, everyone's known it was me from the start. Everyone but you."

"But... but you couldn't have..."

"Why not? Just because Whiffle's 'shoe on a stick' was a hoax? That idiot never got close enough to figure out my methods. I'm sure it was all he could do to come up with another way on his own. A lousy one, at that. The truth is *so* much more delicious."

Through all the astonishment, Horus' sense of betrayal began to congeal into righteous anger. "But this is madness. You can't stand there and tell me all this and think you'll get away with it in the end."

"Who's going to stop me? A good citizen like you? But wouldn't that violate your sacred oath of confidentiality? Wouldn't that fly in the face of your sworn duty to represent your client's wishes? Face it, Horus. Your own ludicrous system demands you go out there tomorrow and clear my good name."

Horus felt more and more out of his depth. That anyone could spew such brazen contempt for... well, seemingly *everything*... had never entered his mind. It was a conversation with an abstraction – an Onyxadon or Wxldlr. "I can't understand," he admitted. "What could turn a man into a monster like you?"

"Why would anyone want to be anything less?" Adam asked with upturned palms. "You're all just afraid, I guess. I wouldn't know any other reason. I used to be afraid, too, truth be told. But then, you know what I found out?"

"What?"

"That the so-called 'long arm of the law' is only as dangerous as the sanctimonious softies out there perpetuating the myth. *People*. People who think of themselves as establishment – who hold themselves to all the rules the best they can – but who change their tune in an instant if they see someone *else* drop the ball. People who would readily excuse all kinds of faults in everyone around them, just as long as they can tell themselves it was a *mistake*. A misunderstanding. A moment of weakness. People who just can't help but feel *sorry* for each other. People a lot like yourself, actually."

Horus frowned. "I don't feel sorry for you. Not anymore. You're a villain. The worst I've ever come across."

"Villain. Heretic. Rebel. Heathen. Visionaries have been called a lot of things over the ages. But I think one day, people are going to wake up and realize they have absolutely no reason to toe the line. No drum to march to but their own. In the meantime, I'll do what I can to show it to them." He turned his wicked chin up confidently. "And you're going to help me, Horus. Because after all: you have to."

* * *

KNOCK KNOCK

"Come in," Deborah called over her shoulder from the dining room table.

Horus turned the knob, opening the door with a creak. "Deborah, I need help. You wouldn't..." He stopped. He thought he could see well enough for himself what she was doing, but he was loath to accept it. "What's all this?" he asked.

"Art's manuscripts," she said. "I'm proofing them for him."

Horus didn't breathe. "You're... what?"

"He was here. I talked with him... maybe an hour or two ago." She turned from her work and shook her head at him. "Horus: He's not doing well."

At a prompt like that, he had to let the issue at hand rest, if only for a moment. "How bad? Tears? Irrational anger?"

"I wish it was just that," she answered. "He was masking it all with crazy optimism. Kept suggesting he and Blucille would 'work it out somehow'. He was totally deluded. It broke my heart just to listen to it. I didn't know what to say most of the time."

Horus shook his head. He hadn't been there, and couldn't really blame her for failing to snap him back to reality, even if he had. But seeing that she'd ultimately taken on some of Art's responsibilities, he couldn't mistake that she'd erred. "And you… let him talk you into doing his work?"

"That was almost the worst part of it," she explained. "I asked him if he was keeping up on his editing alright, and he shrugged it off. Said he didn't really feel like working on it."

He only stared at her. "Deborah… you can't do his work *for* him. Volunteer a bit of help, maybe… but *this*? If it's found out…"

She sighed. "Look, I know it's bad. But all the extra jobs are getting rolled back as we speak. I'm not going to let him get executed over a few hours' heartbroken sloughing off."

"But he *is* sloughing off. It won't matter the reason," Horus insisted. "Deborah, don't you see how serious this is? I know how he must feel. I can't imagine his grief. But he has no excuse… and we can't make excuses for him. What happens if he refuses to do his regular job? You can't enable him like this."

She slumped, heaving a great breath as she ran a hand over her ears. "Honestly, Horus, at this point I'm just hoping he hops his own fishing boat and makes straight for Cape Deltrix."

Horus locked up. This whole conversation was quickly moving from bad to worse. "What did you say?"

She threw her empty hand at the table. "I want him to jump ship, alright? Assume a fake identity and start all over. He can say he's a refugee, or a survivor of a shipwreck. And he and Blucille can quietly pick back up where they left off."

"But he *can't*. Derelict his duty? Lie? Rope Blucille into the deception? Throw away the rulebook just to gratify himself?"

Deborah stood from the table – put her hands on her hips. "That's a little high-minded coming from someone who's moved Heck and earth to buy a few of his clients a second chance, isn't it? Someone who needed a fresh start *himself*, in case you've forgotten. The lives we've left…" She stopped, composing herself. "I just can't believe you'd deny your own friend something like this. After everything you've been through yourself."

"It's not the *same*, Deborah," he said, walking further into the room. "I had to come back to a life of accountability, not turn my back on it. I had to return to society... not foist it off when it wasn't all I wished it to be." He shook his head. "I can't condone this. I can't give Art my blessing to unfetter himself just to pursue some... some *feeling* of his."

Her eyes flared. She took a step back. "Is that all you think this is about, Horus? Just a *feeling*?"

"That *is* all it's about," he replied. "I'm sorry. But that's all there is to it."

She just stood there, frowning. It was a frown Horus had never seen from her before... least of all directed at him. She wasn't merely disagreeing with him anymore. She was disappointed. "You know, Horus... there are times I wonder if you even know what love is."

The words were a knife through his heart. This from the mouth of the woman he loved more than any other person in the world. He *loved* her – truly, and with unflinching devotion. And she didn't even think he knew what that meant. More than that: This apparently wasn't even the first time she'd questioned it. He couldn't dream of a more catastrophic failure on his part. It stung in his chest, and all up and down his throat. He couldn't speak... and that was fortunate. He could only turn to walk away...

...But much as he had earlier that same evening, about the time he reached the door, he found he did have something to say. He remembered his whole reason for coming in the first place. And as his anger with himself turned outward, for better or worse, he spoke. "He's guilty, you know."

Deborah turned glistening eyes back up at him. "What?"

"Adam. He's the jaywalker. I don't know how, but he's the one. He told me so himself."

She managed to be astonished. "He... confessed?"

"Boasted, more like it. Flaunted it to my face. Turns out all this time I've been representing the worst criminal this city's ever seen. He did it all – for no motive outside of pure Malum In Se. I never imagined anyone could see things the ugly way he does. He's every bit the megalomaniac from the people's most whimsical fears. And that would've been enough all on its own, without having to hear you echo half of what he said just now. After all, his advice for Art was the same as yours."

Deborah didn't have any answer for that. She only looked away crossly. Horus felt no better for having lashed out. But there was nothing more for it. He had to get out of there to staunch the hole he was digging. He left, hating himself. At a time when he should've been tender, he'd only found it in his heart to be the voice of reason at its most bitter and uncaring. He'd failed Art. He'd failed Deborah. He'd salved nothing. Yes – the only person he was any help to at all was a monster.

* * *

As if the long night could've known any more unwelcome twists, Horus intuited that he was walking into yet another one as he neared his home. Standing sentinel in his front yard was a man who – from a distance in the dark – appeared to be a complete stranger. As he drew closer, though – heedless of any thought of danger – Horus discovered that it was only Gord.

"There you are, Mr. Templar," Gord said. "Fine night for stargazing."

"I wouldn't know," Horus replied, dimly recalling such vapid trifles as stars and sky. "What brings you here, Gord?"

"A bit of bad news, I'm afraid."

"I do believe that's the only kind," he said with a sigh. "What is it?"

"I'm not going to be working for you anymore."

On the spectrum of bad news, Horus couldn't help welcoming this latest revelation as quite dull. He already knew the employment boom was being rescinded, and it wasn't as if he and Gord had grown all that close over the few days they'd technically worked together. Probably the worst thing about it was being obliged now to sound politely disappointed. "I'm... sorry to hear that, Gord," he offered. "But I wish you well with... um... whatever it is you customarily do."

"Hm," Gord mused. "Unfortunately, I don't think that's going to work out, either. The extra jobs... the railway overhaul... even the theme park, which seemed like a sure winner... all busts. Oh, I guess I can't be too disappointed about the double-decker bikes, though. The irony is with all the extra work to do, almost no one had the luxury of traveling anywhere in tandem. On top of that, I guess there ended up being a lot of arguments about who had to ride on the second story. Still, they sold reasonably well."

Suddenly, the news wasn't so dull anymore. Horus' eyes bulged, and not for the first time that day. "You... but that means you're... the Royal Comptroller? Sidon Thangorodrim?"

"I guess I never mentioned that, did I?" he asked, watching his fingernails as he rubbed his thumb against their edges. "Never liked going by my full name. Too clunky. Besides, there's something cerebral about a good, short nickname. You just have to be clever enough to pick one that fits."

"But that means..." Horus hesitated to say the words. "That means you're going to be executed. Gord... I really am terribly sorry."

He just kept looking off in his thoughtfully detached way. "I appreciate that, Mr. Templar. I'm not wild about it myself. But, that's how the story goes. Royal Comptroller is a volatile position. Always has been. Odds were good it would come to this sooner or later. I might've liked to try out a few more things, but it seems I've already overplayed my hand. I'm content knowing I learned a valuable lesson: If you set out to change the world, don't change it all at once. It only leads to trouble."

"Well... it's nice to see you're taking it so well," Horus said, very much at a loss for anything else to say. "You're a most peculiar person, Gord. I wish the Czarina had seen fit to let you put the valuable lesson you've learned into practice."

Gord looked at him with a grin. "Much obliged. But now, I suppose I'd better get going. Undoubtedly, they're waiting for me."

Horus nodded in return – a drawn-back look on his own face. "Undoubtedly."

"Goodbye, Horus – if I may call you Horus."

"Goodbye... Gord."

As they began to part ways, Horus could only resolve to go inside and help himself to a few generous spoonfuls of lard, a great big stemmed glass of grape juice, and then climb into bed, where his psyche could wrestle with oblivion for a few hours. But before he could do any of that, Gord called out again...

"Horus: one last thing."

"Yes?"

"I really would keep a close eye on that client of yours, if I were you. Something about him doesn't sit right... if you know what I mean."

"I begin to. Thank you, Gord. I'll take that into consideration."

Gord nodded, turned, and walked away. This time, Horus watched him go, marveling as he arrived at a unifying thesis for the day: He didn't know people half as well as he thought he did.

Chapter 15

Scrii-scratch... scrii-scratch... scrii-scratch...

Whenever Art simply couldn't stand to look at the pale, sunken-in face of Steward Jamison any longer, his gaze would inevitably wander off to the mesmerizing flicks of the EKG machine they'd hooked him up to countless hours ago. In a way, he was grateful for its mind-numbing rhythm. But at the same time, no matter how long he watched it make the exact same scratch, the exact same way – over, and over, and over again – he never truly relaxed, knowing the next scratch could be bigger, and stronger... or what seemed much more likely: slower, and slighter. Once – an eternity ago – he'd made an effort to amuse himself with the fact that this was the same crazy gizmo Jamison had used in one of his 'techniques' during their big case together. But at a time like this, any irony worth a chuckle would inevitably leave a bitter aftertaste for hours to come. It was a miserable place to be – a dark, cold room that smelled of bleach, where the only sound was of the needles on the paper. Even so, Art couldn't presently imagine being anywhere else. It wasn't just that he knew he *should* be, for Jamison's sake – the only kind of obligation that could even touch him at present. No, besides that, he knew that Jamison's was the only company he felt he belonged in. If the old Detective was to pull through, then Art absolutely needed to be there to see it – to see that people *do* pull through. But if he didn't... well, either way, he might as well have confirmation. In the meantime, they were two of a kind. Two men with hardly a hope between them. Two men whose very lives hung by a thread...

"Come on, Jamison," he said quietly, as he did every so often. "You've just gotta make it."

Suddenly, he was aware of the dull clatter of boots in the hall, and the rise and fall of an argument already in progress. His ears lifted to meet the approaching sound, and even though there were many rooms in the infirmary wing, he knew instinctively the distant voices were coming for Jamison. A sleeping or otherwise inert Dr. Nokkaeru – who was perched in the corner – swiveled her head as she too took notice. And before long, they all came bursting into the room.

"How many more ways could he possibly have brought this on himself?" the first voice demanded; it turned out to be the voice of High Constable Amadeus. "He wouldn't desist when commanded, and when we came to arrest him, he fled. It was *his* choice to forego due process and accelerate his sentencing. So tell me why in the Sam Heck we're trying so hard to keep a guy like that breathing?!"

"The same woulds't be done with any who resisteth arrest, Lord," Miloje countered. "So long as he perisheth not, he may yet standeth trial. Due process doth demand this wherever possible."

"What? And give him a highly public opportunity to get up and cast doubt on Brocksmith's guilt? Can't you see that if he'd died on the street it would've been the biggest break we could get? That pulling the plug now would save us from countless troubles later?" By now, he was standing over Jamison, trying to make sense of all the paraphernalia on and around him. His eyes settled on the electrocardiogram. "What's this thing? Is this what's keeping his heart going?"

"It only measures its impulses, you buffoon," Nokkaeru answered, circling in.

Amadeus – a man not accustomed to being addressed in this way – was noticeably unimpressed. "You'd better watch that attitude, Bird, or you'll wind up like your patient."

Far from cowering, Nokkaeru craned her head up as high as she could on her long neck to meet him. "Strong words from a weak mind. You will not lay a finger on me *or* my patient."

"Insolent...!" he barked. "Do you have any idea who you're talking to? I am the Lord High Constable of Jast-Madiir! I'll do whatever I darn well please!"

"Then it may please you to consider who it is *you* are speaking to, *lord*," she recited back. "I am an esteemed envoy and decorated medical professional of Roemnar." She tilted her beak in a mocking sort of way. "You're in the business of warfare, High Constable. Care to instigate one with *my* home country?"

Amadeus could only stand there with his big lip creasing his small one. Finally, he turned his argument back to open forum. "This is nothing short of infectious insanity! Here's a man known to spend his days beating confessions out of random passersby, breaking the windows out of his own house and etching gibberish all over the walls in his basement. And you're all standing up for him! A certifiable maniac!"

"If he be certifiable, Lord, then letteth him be *certified*," Miloje put back in. "I maketh my appeal only to procedure."

As they went on arguing, Art became dead to it. To him, it was just a lot of noise. He wished they'd stop and go away, and leave Jamison in peace. But what could he do about it? Nothing.

...But then, as his attention regressed back to the EKG, he noticed something. He blinked hard, not believing at first. But it was unmistakable. The needles were spiking...

"Hey... hey, Doc," he called – weakly, at first. "I think that..."

Jamison shot up from the bed, his huge eyes fixing straight into Art's as he reached out and tethered himself to him with one shaky hand, pulling out his air tube with the other. Then, with a hoarse whisper, and a paralyzing look of absolute conviction, he said these words:

"I am secretly evil."

Immediately thereafter, he collapsed.

Everyone watched him breathlessly. Long seconds passed. There was no more sign from Steward Jamison.

Art couldn't accept it. He couldn't believe this was what all the waiting and hoping against hope had come to. But it was no use. The needles didn't so much as twitch anymore.

"What a pity," a new voice said with a sigh. "But I suppose it only goes to prove the High Constable's point. The man was mad."

Art turned around slowly, finding the newcomer standing behind him. "Dr. Creevey?"

"Lias, please," Creevey insisted. "That is, I hope what I'm about to say won't come between us, Art. I can see you considered Detective Jamison a colleague, and a man worthy of respect. And I'm remiss to speak badly of the dead. But Art: He wasn't the good man you think he was."

"What do you mean?" Art asked. "What are you even doing here, Lias?"

"Presenting the findings of my investigation, I'm afraid," he answered. "You see, I had a look at this wall of his." He shook his head dejectedly. "I don't dare repeat half the twists and tangles that were in that man's head. It was the biggest mess I've seen since the Syzygy case. The only thing I found that was even close to a coherent MO was an uncontrollable urge to spread mayhem."

"But... that can't be," Art practically whimpered.

"Of course it can," Amadeus scoffed. "The man clawed his way back from the threshold of death just to tell you he was evil. What more do you need to see? If that's not certifiable insanity, I don't know what is."

"I take no joy in doing it, but I'd be willing to submit as much to the board myself," Creevey suggested.

"I'd thank you to do that." Amadeus slapped a strong hand on Creevey's shoulder. "You've done good work here today, Doctor. It's about time this was all finally laid to rest."

Creevey and Amadeus made their exit. Miloje lingered just long enough to sullenly remove his police bobby, before he too departed. Art had no mind to go anywhere. He just kept on staring at Jamison's lifeless body, as if a prolonged enough meditation on the sight would somehow grant him the power to make sense of it all.

"I am sorry, Friend Mallard," Nokkaeru consoled him, after a prolonged silence, so that he was almost surprised to find she was still there in the room with him. "Undoubtedly you are disappointed that your investigation should come to this unsatisfactory conclusion. As indeed, I regret that my surgical efforts were ultimately fruitless."

"Yeah," he said. "There's that. But mostly, I'm sad that he's dead."

"Ah, that too is a misfortune," she admitted. "But sundering and loss are the lament of lesser minds than your own. Prithee do not mourn the inevitable any longer than you must."

Worse than merely unhelpful, her words inspired a sudden dread in him. He realized he couldn't imagine an end to his mourning. "Doc, I gotta tell ya: il's all getting ta be more than a guy can take. Like everything's just falling apart on me all at once."

"You have other troubles?" she asked. "Why don't you tell me about them? I have certain qualifications."

He had no reservation about spilling the whole sad story right then and there, but drudging up the words themselves was a grief. "Doc... it's Blucille. She's, uh... sh-she's gone. Transferred to Cape Deltrix."

Nokkaeru made no immediate response. He thought maybe she was reaching down deep for healing words of wisdom. But then, she started to chuckle. "Is *that* all? Friend Mallard – don't you see what good fortune this is? You have been spared a most compromising joy. Would that I had lately been so blessed myself!"

"But..." He faltered. "But I love her."

"But of course you do," Nokkaeru agreed with a nod. "That is precisely what makes her sudden departure so fortuitous. Love has an awful way of distorting one's priorities – of reinforcing all the wrong emotions. Happiness, where there ought to be acrimony. Care, where there ought to be callousness. I know it's hard now, but you will soon see: It really is much better this way."

Art stood up, shaking his head. "That's a hard wrap, Doc. A real hard wrap. Don't get me wrong – I'm sure you're smart enough in your own way. But you've got a lot ta learn when it comes ta this."

He started to walk away, to her immediate bewilderment. "But… what have I said? Where are you going?"

"I dunno. But I guess I'm done here."

Passing into the hall and shoving his hands in his pockets, Art was well on his way to shutting out the world around him when he heard rapid steps in the distance again. He managed to be just curious enough to look up and see who it was. He found Captain Alexei barreling up to him.

"Mr. Mallard – I've just received word! The High Constable! Has he been…?"

"Here and gone," Art interjected. "You're a little late ta the party, Long Legs. There's nothing left ta see."

Alexei's eyes were still wide with immediacy. "But, Detective Jamison? What has become of him? I do hope his Excellency didn't…"

"He didn't have to. Jamison woke up, said he was secretly evil, and bit the dust. End of story."

The Captain shook his head. "But that makes no sense."

"Nothing makes sense anymore, Sirens." He started walking away again.

"Then… our hopes of catching the mole?" Alexei pressed just the same. "They've come to nothing in the end?"

"Yup," he replied, not looking back. "Score another one for the bad guys."

* * *

Looking over to the table across from him, Horus had to pity the young Mesomela scrambling with the contents of his briefcase. A green addition to the St. Argonsburg team of ADAs, Horus seemed to recall his name was Darius. The poor fellow looked as if whatever he was searching for must've been left in an altogether different briefcase. It really was a sorry sight.

Against his better judgment, Horus' gaze wandered the other way, finding Deborah with her eyes turned down at her watch.

"You don't have to do that anymore, you know."

"I know," she replied, going right on doing it. "I'm actually trying to ignore you this time."

Horus suppressed an eye-roll. This being the first time he'd ever earned Deborah's ire, he wouldn't have known what to expect, but childish snippiness wasn't it. Still, at least he had a sure indication that their tiff from the night before hadn't simply blown over on its own. He'd have to make it right somehow. It would have to be handled carefully, though. An apology struck him as overreaching. The last thing he needed was to make it sound like he'd changed his position. But what did that leave? He didn't really know.

Even so, he had to try.

"Deborah… I regret that what I said last night came out so indelicately. Maybe I didn't make it very clear, but I was afraid. Afraid of the direction things seemed to be going in, and the rate they were headed that way. Emotions were running so high. I didn't want to see you, or Art, get carried away."

Her eyes shifted his way; her frown looked less sharp, and more sad. "Maybe my idea *was* a little rash. I can appreciate you wanting to protect us. It's just that you made his heartache sound so small. Unimportant."

"It *isn't* small," Horus replied. "I understand the enormity of what he's going through. Better than you seem to think I do. I've faced grievous losses before. I know what a defining moment that can be. But the bottom line is, he's going to have to find it in himself to move on from Blucille. There's just no other conscionable choice."

"I don't think he should just *give up*."

"Yet that may be exactly what he *must* do."

She shook her head, sighing. "I'm sorry, Horus, but it sounds like we'll have to agree to disagree on this one."

The prospect made him blanch. "We've never done *that* before."

"Believe me, I don't like it any better than you do."

All of a sudden – whether because of a hush in the gallery too subtle to register, a chill in the air, or some other alarm at the approach of evil that transcended the traditional senses – they both turned to find Adam on approach to the defense table.

"Well, here we go," Deborah intoned. "Nothing like having to sit beside a psychopath to make the day even brighter. Do you think it's too late to have this changed to an *In Absentia* case?"

"For once I think I'd be completely okay with that," Horus quipped.

As he got closer, they tried to appear indifferent about it. If they could simply avoid looking at him, maybe it would make what they had to do at least a little easier. Horus heard him sit down. He could feel the eye on him. It made his fur crawl... until finally, he seemed to have no choice but to turn, finding Adam smiling at him.

"Good morning, Horus. Ready for the big day?"

He shifted his attention back to the fore. "Don't test me, Adam. I could still decide to throw this thing."

"Oh, come on, now. I think I know you better than that. Good people like you always try their best."

He could feel his jowls adhering to his teeth. "As a matter of fact, I'm trying my best right now."

"Aw, you're *really* having a hard time with this, aren't you? Would it help if I said I was *sorry*?"

Horus shot him a scalding look. But before he had time to say anything, the bailiff called out...

"All rise for the Honorable Judge Thutmose."

Horus rose on cue. "We'll continue this discussion later," he boded quietly.

"I wouldn't be too sure of that. Later, I'll be free."

Thutmose took his seat, and the court convened. "We begin with an obligatory bit of side-business," he announced. "Since last we adjourned, Assistant District Attorney Cordon has been transferred to a new jurisdiction. She will be replaced by Assistant District Attorney Darius." He looked down at the young prosecutor, finding him still quietly sifting through his papers. "Mr. Prosecutor?"

Darius turned his wide eyes up at the bench. "Uh, yes, Sir? Your Honor, I mean?"

"Are you quite prepared to assume this responsibility?"

"...Well, that is, it's kind of a lot on short notice, and I *am* pretty new, so hopefully..."

"Are you *prepared*?" Thutmose interjected, raising a brow.

"Yes, your Honor," Darius composed himself to say. It seemed at last he was able to pick up what Thutmose was putting down.

"Very well. Then we move on to the defense's case. Proceed, Mr. Templar."

Horus turned to the gallery. "I call Sergeant Basil to the stand."

* * *

"Now, Sergeant Basil, this will be brief; I have only one line of questioning for you," Horus began, pacing the floor. "You testified that you saw the offending shoeprint on the ground. Would you please describe the quality of the print?"

Basil cleared his throat. "The quality? I'm not sure I understand."

"Well, how much of the tread actually left a visible imprint on the cobblestone?"

"All of it – or quite nearly," Basil replied.

"So you would say it was a *very* distinct print? Unmistakably made by a full shoe, and not just – say – the heel?"

"Yes, certainly. As I indicated it was very much in line with the infamous tales – with the reports of the other incidents, perhaps I should say. Left Foot Lazarus made his mark quite clear and visible."

"I see," Horus said with a nod. "Thank you, Sergeant. That will be all."

After a moment, Thutmose shot an angry look at Darius. "*Mr. Prosecutor*," he called out sternly.

Darius froze in the midst of yet more shuffling. "No-questions-on-cross," he couldn't say fast enough.

"Very well. The witness may step down."

Even as Basil did so, Deborah took this as her cue to get up, round the table, and begin unrolling an enormous piece of paper on the ground.

Thutmose pointed dubiously with his pen. "What is it your secretary is engaging in here, Mr. Templar?"

"If the court please, the testimony I'm about to introduce will require a visual demonstration."

"Not many will be able to see a roll of paper on the floor," the judge pointed out. "You ought to have procured an easel."

Horus shook his head. "I'm afraid this test will have to be made against the floor. It's the only way to ensure the accuracy of the results."

Deborah popped open a can of paint.

"I'm unsure of this," Thutmose said.

Almost too late, Horus recognized something of a gambit. Duty constrained him to follow through with his case so long as he was able. But what if the judge were to stop him before he could even begin? "Unfortunately, I will also have to deface Prosecution Exhibit-A. I understand that this is most regrettable and improper, but the experiment demands it. Of course... it can only be done with your Honor's permission."

Thutmose contemplated, stroking the sides of his snout. "Well... I'm not entirely..."

"Oh! But Mr. Templar! You mustn't leave me out! Tell him you mean to call an expert witness to the stand! Surely that will account for something."

Thutmose rapped his gavel. "We will have no outbursts! Who dares to address the court in this fashion?"

"It was I, your Honor," Forasius spoke up, standing and bowing his head. "My sincere apologies. I shouldn't have let my personal investiture in this discovery cause me to speak out so."

"A Heron Plague Doctor," Thutmose recounted to himself. He turned to Horus. "This is to be your witness?"

"Yes, your Honor," he was obliged to answer.

Thutmose resumed his repose. "The intellectual eminence of Plague Doctors is much to be respected," he said. "So be it. You may proceed, Mr. Templar."

Another first. Horus found himself dratting Forasius' pluck.

* * *

"Here then is the crux of the matter," Forasius summed up his testimony at last. "You cannot with a mere stick under your arm faithfully simulate the Human stride: the weight distribution – the many points of articulation. Attached this way, you can only apply pressure to the heel of the shoe. You would never achieve a good, full print such as the Sergeant described."

"Alright," Horus replied. "Thank you, Dr. Forasius."

Forasius nodded. "I am most pleased to have been of service, Sir."

Horus stepped away, feeling a bit of relief wash over him. Forasius' testimony – though impeaching to the prosecution's entire case in its content – seemed to have practically flown over the gallery, what with all its longwinded and specialized jargon. Perhaps if he could make a quick getaway now, the significance of Forasius' examination would only be hazily remembered when it came time to reach the verdict. "Cross examine," he called out casually.

"One moment, Mr. Templar," Thutmose ordered. "You seem to have neglected your demonstration."

Horus was stopped in his tracks. "Of course. How foolish of me." He had the misfortune of looking right at Adam, who smiled and made a little scooting motion with his hand as if to say, 'go on, now'. "I will require the assistance of the bailiff, as well as Mr. Bradley Hanover."

"So ordered," Thutmose assented.

The bailiff came forward, as well as Brad Hanover – a local paperboy of about 10-12 years who, Horus had learned, wore size 6. Horus set him up with a fresh shoe that he explained to the court matched in every way the make of the one on the end of the polearm apparatus. Then, after carefully dipping the shoe in a shallow trough filled with red paint, he had the lad step on the paper. The print, of course, was full and distinct. He then had the bailiff try to recreate the stamp in blue with Exhibit-A under his arm. The bailiff – a strategically chosen party who obviously wouldn't have been in Horus' camp – positively demonstrated his desire to prove the Plague Doctor wrong by making multiple attempts. But try as he might – with concentration progressing to frustration written all over his face – the man never arrived at the print he was hoping for. Not by a wide margin.

"My goodness," Thutmose said, arrested by a good long look at the results. "Mr. Templar – you must bring up your test where the whole court can see."

Judging by the judge's reaction, he wished he didn't have to. "It is rather difficult, your Honor. I have only the one arm. The paper will roll shut. Is it not enough that your Honor sees the results?"

"No indeed. They all must see for themselves." He gestured back at the defense table. "Enlist the aid of your secretary, if you must."

Horus looked at Deborah. She stood, mirroring his expression. But she came round, and the two of them obliged Thutmose's command.

Once the gallery laid eyes on the sheet, the room was filled with the strained whisper of their amazement. All around the one good red shoe print they found a dozen or so shabby heel marks and narrow bands in blue. It didn't take an expert in podiatry to unravel the significance of a stark image like this. The 'physical evidence' in the case had been a shallow fiction all along. The shoe on the stick was never more than a red herring.

Horus and Deborah surely looked just as astonished as everyone else, such was their horror at what was sure to happen next. As the crowd was permitted to continue in their outburst, sans admonishment from the judge, Horus' gaze inevitably fell on Adam's unabashed look of pure self-satisfaction. There were no two ways about it. He'd just won the most sinister man he'd ever met a sure acquittal.

Chapter 16

Deborah folded the newspaper down grimly, shaking her head. "Well, there you go. It's not even in here."

"Unbelievable," Horus said, slumping on the piano bench. "I don't think total suppression is quite in the spirit of Hamilton's original plan to downplay the significance of the case. I can't imagine a louder silence."

"I mean, I can appreciate their problem," Deborah allowed. "People find out Adam was acquitted, they'll either wonder why the State couldn't make the charges stick, or they might even entertain the possibility that he *was* innocent, and the State was on the wrong track from the start. The administration gets egg on its face either way."

"And the real truth is darker still. It's a synthesis of all the worst possibilities. They *were* on the wrong track, even if they had the right man. With what they had to go on, they couldn't prove he was guilty." He reached for a handy glass of grape juice. "Even *I* couldn't prove he was guilty, if I was in their place. I still have no idea how he did it. He needed to be able to wear a size 6 shoe. But we saw with our own eyes he couldn't."

"It has to be something simple. A shoe with a false sole glued over the real one?"

He shook his head. "The department left no stone unturned at the crime scene. He couldn't have stashed anything without their finding it. They even found something he *didn't* stash. And obviously, he wasn't wearing anything of the sort when they found him."

She thought for a moment. "What about magic? Seeing as that's a thing now."

"There *is* some interesting magic out there; I've seen it for myself. Up, Down – Positive, Negative. But *Size* magic? There aren't even any corresponding Dianodes. No, I don't think it was magic."

"What are we going to do? We can't let him get away with it."

"He *did* get away with it."

For a long time, there were no words. Even as the debate ended in just such a way to remind them of other debates they still had on the shelf, there didn't seem anything left to say... and even if there was, neither one of them wanted to say it. But finally, Horus remembered the reason he was currently sitting in ambush at the Ecre Point place, and decided to broach it...

"You're sure this is a good idea? What if he doesn't like what I have to say any better than you did?"

"Horus, you *have* to do this," she appealed. "He's your friend, and you have to talk to him. Let him know you're there for him. He needs that reassurance right now. It can't be put off." She looked at him somewhat pleadingly. "Just... please: If you feel you have to advise him, do it gently."

Horus was inclined to accept that as worse than a jab. He thought he'd proven well enough when they discussed it in court that he *was* sympathetic. But apparently, he was such an unfeeling person that she practically had to beg him to be sensitive. "I'll do my best."

Fortuitously, Art came ambling down the stairs, just then. It wasn't a slow plod. More of a chipper stroll, which Art complimented with an easy expression that could've passed for sincere. Horus felt his gut twist.

"Hey, Debs; hey, Horus," Art said, gently knocking on his own door frame. "Mind if I come in?"

"Hello, Art," Horus replied, gesturing at the room. "Please – make yourself at home."

"Heh, right," Art chuckled, picking up on the irony. "I'll see what I can do."

As he moved into the room, Deborah started on her way out. "I think I'll leave you boys to catch up for a while. See you in a bit."

Horus stared blankly at her. In fairness, if she'd stayed, he might've been miffed that she felt the need to moderate him. Still, watching her retreat immediately upset him even more. He tried to think of some subtle way of catching her in her own words – suggesting that he'd be sure to louse things up even worse without her help. But his cleverness failed him, and he suddenly realized the whole reason he didn't want her to go was because deep down, he *didn't* feel he could handle the pressure of talking to Art on his own – something she'd already had to do once. In the end, he said nothing.

"I see you're already into the vintage, Horus," Art said, rounding the bar. "Think I'll have me a glass myself. Want me ta top ya off? I'm opening the good stuff. *359* – fresh off the vine. Can't beat it." He popped the cork. "This was an engagement present, ya know."

Horus' throat seized up. He looked at Deborah again just as she was reaching the threshold. They exchanged pained glances, but she continued on, leaving Horus to postulate the sure ruin that lay ahead.

"So... Deborah said you wanted to talk to me?"

For the third time in rapid succession, Horus was dumbstricken. He hadn't considered that Deborah would lure Art here on no pretense whatsoever. "Uh, yes. I did."

"Okay. What about?" he asked nonchalantly. As if he couldn't have guessed.

Horus was quickly feeling buried in all the layers of this charade. He did all he could think to do and stood up. "Well, of course..." He got stuck right away. Fortunately, the surge of pressure made it impossible to be anything but plain-spoken. "Art: I am so terribly sorry about Blucille. That the two of you should be separated like this... well... it's among the most heinous twists of fate I've ever known. I regret that I haven't had a chance to tell you in person."

Art gave a sudden laugh. "What? *That*?" He waved it off as he sat down with his drink. "Peanuts. Don't sweat it, Horus. I don't let any a-that bother me anymore."

"You... you don't?"

"Nah. Oh, sure, there's been some ups and downs. I was upset, at first. Who wouldn't be? But ya see, this is our *thing*. We get put up against impossible odds, and we beat 'em every time. I don't know how yet, but I know we'll lick this one, too. I mean, for cryin' out loud! We went through all that other stuff. Nobody goes through all that, only ta fall flat on their face in the end. Am I right?"

The loaded question. Horus could only imagine if Deborah had been there to see him put up to it. What was he to do? He *wanted* to be reassuring. He wanted it more than anything. But he couldn't play into the lunacy. He couldn't deceive his friend by letting him deceive himself. "Art... I think you have to consider the possibility that..."

There was another knock in the doorway. It seemed for a moment that Deborah was there to 'save him' after all. But when Horus turned, he didn't find who he expected to...

"Excuse me, Sirs," a policeman said. "I understand this is an alternative residence of Artimus Mallard?"

"Nope," Art replied. "This is an alternative *office* for Horus Templar."

Horus blinked. "You're not actually giving it to me?"

"If it's such an open secret that the whole department knows about it, I don't see the point of keeping it anymore," Art said with a shrug. "It's practically your place already. I'm not doing ya any big favors."

"But then, you *are* Artimus Mallard, aren't you?" the policeman interjected.

"Yeah, that's me."

"Then I must ask you to come back with me to Civil Headquarters at once. There's been an incident. We have strong indication it may be in connection with your case – the matter of the mole. Much as we've tried to close the ordeal, the villain has reopened it himself. It seems he's struck again."

Horus and Art exchanged a look. "Well, there ya go," Art framed it. "See, Horus? About the time ya give up hope on something, it's back on again." He turned to the officer. "Sure, I'll come with ya. Can't think of anything better ta do right now anyway."

"I'd like to come along as well, if that's permitted," Horus offered. He was curious what was going on, of course. But more than that, Horus felt the need to keep an eye on Art. Whether he was just bitter, or worse – actually expecting all his problems to go away magically – he was far from himself.

"I don't believe Mr. Blackforest would object," the policeman answered. "Come now. The trail runs cold."

They fell in step behind him, Horus quickly succumbing to a flurry of questions. "What sort of trail are we on, Sergeant?"

"A gravely embarrassing one, Mr. Templar. I'm afraid there's been an escape."

"An escape?" Horus marveled. "From the detention area? Was it that Lieutenant Carbine? But I thought he'd already been sent back to the barracks."

The Sergeant shook his head. "Not Carbine. It was someone much worse."

* * *

"Who was on guard duty when this happened?!" Blackforest demanded as he, Miloje, and an obviously overwhelmed Captain Huxley careened to the depths of Civil HQ.

"I honestly don't know, Sir," Huxley was forced to admit. "All the personnel schedules seem to have been disposed of. We can't even be sure when the escape took place."

"Well, that's about what I should expect." Blackforest curled his great claws into dangerously tight fists. "Someone's head is going to roll for this! I guess it's going to be mine."

"With respect, Hamilton, this is no time to play the blame-game," Miloje imparted. "Before all else, we should concern ourselves with how the prisoner got out."

"Not that it's any excuse, of course," Huxley spoke up, "but couldn't he have... I don't know... used his powers?"

"Ridiculous!" Blackforest exclaimed. "As if we weren't forced to take every precaution! There hasn't been a timepiece allowed down there in months!"

Miloje suddenly stopped walking. They all took notice.

"What is it, Stenya?" Blackforest asked.

"The answer to the riddles, perhaps," Miloje mused. "We supposed he needed the pocket watches to weave his mesmerizing web. What if he never did? What if he's been at liberty to come and go all along?"

Huxley and Blackforest regarded him with wide eyes. "What are you suggesting, Sir?" Huxley asked, at length. "He's just been biding his time?"

Miloje shook his head. "No. I think perhaps he's been quite busy."

"You can't mean?" Blackforest said.

"But why not? It fits everything. Jamison's own investigation suggested it was someone quite low in the department. *Subterranean*, he said. Who lower than a prisoner?"

"But how would he know about the magic shipment? How would...?" He stopped himself.

"You begin to see it now, don't you? If he had free reign of our minds, he could've learned *anything*. From any one of us. Anyone who had been down there and passed him by in the last few months."

Blackforest shook his head, resuming his march down into the detention area. "I have to see the cell."

Just as they reached the doors to the dungeon, another officer sprung up in their way. "Mr. Blackforest! Deputy Constable! There's been a shocking development!"

"If you don't think we've already heard about it, you need your head examined," Blackforest waved him off, hardly slowing down. "Now make yourself useful and show us the cell. We have to find *something* there. Something that'll point us to him. We *can't* let him get away!"

"But Sir, he hasn't!" the officer exclaimed. They turned to look at him. "He's back."

They all exchanged faces of astonishment. "Back?"

"Yes, Sir." The officer swallowed. "Right where we left him."

* * *

The small desk lamp in the interrogation room flickered, casting its frantic light on grim, statuesque faces. No one stirred. No one flinched. But for each one of them, the stern expression was at least in part to mask a creeping fear. It was hard enough to demand the truth of a villain they knew they couldn't trust. But in the presence of the *Bishop*... how much could they even trust themselves?

"Don't everyone ask his question all at once, now," Sabracore chuckled, turning up the spades of a few of his shackled tentacles. "This certainly *is* a welcome change from when I first came here, and you all tried to ignore me. Suddenly it seems I have quite the captive audience. Still, I'd hate to do *all* the talking myself. Come on. Any takers?"

"Where did you go?" Horus was the first to venture.

"Ah, Horus Templar," Sabracore doted. "You see? I thought we'd meet again. Not that it's any of your business, but if you must know, I had an appointment to keep. A reckoning with a rather dissatisfied sponsor, you might say."

"A sponsor?" Blackforest asked. "Who are you talking about?"

"And now, the District Attorney chooses his debut question. Bad choice, Mr. Blackforest. It wouldn't matter if I told you. It's not a name you people would know." He pivoted slightly, and it seemed he was considering Captain Alexei with some bright-flashing amusement. "But then again, I suppose *one* of you would."

Alexei looked down, dispirited. Horus watched him with wondering eyes. But Blackforest pressed on.

"You can save your hints and suggestions. Let's get right down to the bottom line. Are you the mole? Have you been selling classified information out of this department?"

Sabracore laughed. "Well, wouldn't that be expedient for you? Finding out the hypnotist you thought you had under lock and key has been mining secrets all along? It's a compelling idea, to be sure. An alarming one. What could I have learned? How much have I been manipulating things to suit my own ends? So many big questions."

Blackforest punched the desk, standing up. "I already asked a question. You *will* answer it."

"And how do you propose to make me, Mr. Blackforest? Torture? Death threats? Please. Or, maybe you think you can force the answers out with your courtroom stare? Are you *sure* you can match minds with me?" He shook his body as one might shake his head. "I wouldn't try it, if I were you."

"I'll do whatever I have to do to protect this department and this city."

"That's a conceit, and you know it. St. Argonsburg is already dead on its feet. You built your foundation on lies... and now, the walls are starting to crumble. You'll see it, soon enough: all the telltale signs. It starts simple. Murmurs of discontent. Eroding confidence. A few outliers committing audacious crimes. You'll try to push back with the only thing you know: more falsehoods. More lies. But you'll only accelerate the rot. You'll face rebellion, and revolt. And ultimately, revolution." He floated back into a bemused posture. "Yes, Mr. Blackforest, this city's judgment day is coming soon. And when it does, I'll be the one holding the gavel."

Blackforest whirled for a handy posse of big, stout policemen, eyes aflame. "Get him out of here. Lock him back up and have the entire detention area quarantined."

"Yes, Sir..." the men said, before leaping into action. Horus could see they were terrified. Terrified it wouldn't be enough. He looked over at Art, who'd averted his eyes, and was taking shallow breaths – driven by sheer nerves to the point of panting. Horus reached out and patted him on the shoulder – the only thing he could think to do. He admired Art for facing so much fear simply by being there, even if he'd done it out of his present pretense of indifference.

Once the Bishop was gone, Blackforest collapsed back in his seat, sighing. "Well, what's the verdict? You all heard what I heard. Is Sabracore our mole? Is there any reasonable doubt?"

No one was quick to answer.

"I stand by the idea," Miloje said at last. "It's certainly more elegant than the notion that the mole was someone *else*, who was able to arrange for the Bishop's comings and goings. He has extraordinary means, and the wish to do us harm. In any case, I feel distinctly that we've underestimated him. We ought to remedy that however we can."

"I concur," Horus said. "It's not something I enjoy recounting, but I do remember my first meeting with the Bishop. In only a few very short moments, he nearly had me giving him my watch. You'll probably remember the incident, since it gave rise to the no-watch policy in the detention area. I, for one, haven't been able to forget it. It felt like more than a polite request he was making. I believe there *was* a certain power in his voice alone. Maybe more so than I knew."

"Whatever you can come up with ta do ta that guy is okay by me," Art put in. "Mole or no mole, he's a varmint. That's for darn sure."

That left only one opinion unvoiced. They all waited in vain for him to say something. "What do you think, Alexei?" Blackforest finally asked.

"I fear to say the question of the mole is now rather moot," he answered, a shaky hand smoothing out his sideburns.

They were all taken aback. "What makes you say that?" Blackforest pressed on quietly.

Alexei stood up, mustering. "Come to my office. There's something you all must see."

* * *

The light from the outside world was pale – cold. Even so, Alexei drew up to his window, looking out as if to search the sky for so much as a single warm glimmer. After a moment, he relented the search, gazing down in thought as he cupped his hand over his chin.

"Well, here we are," Miloje announced. "Pray tell why we've been summoned here, and soon. I've had my fill of mystery."

"You'll find it in my desk," Alexei answered. "First drawer on the right."

They all had to gauge each other's interest in being the one to make the search. Finally, Horus went for it. He walked over, opened the drawer, and right at the top, he found something very strange. An envelope – but not by any means an ordinary envelope. It had no postage... no return address. It was completely unmarked, except for a crimson wax seal – a frightful series of fanning jaws and sharp crescents engulfing a coin. And the paper wasn't white. It was obsidian.

"What is this?"

"Blackmail, Mr. Templar," Alexei explained. "I received it this very morning... as if out of the folds of time. It pains me to say I've seen the like before. Only then, I was never the recipient."

Miloje snapped his fingers. "But this is the just the same as *your* case! The one you unraveled so brilliantly that I felt I had to promote you!"

"Not so brilliantly after all, it seems." Alexei turned back into the room to face them. "For it *is* the same. Down to the last detail of the wax seal. Miloje: I failed. I don't know how, but I failed. And now, it's come back to haunt me. It's followed me to the very capital of Jast-Madiir."

They all seemed to take a moment to digest this. But apart from the thousand-foot-view Miloje had given him in passing some time ago, Horus knew nothing about the case in question. "I'm not sure I can arrive at the full significance of all this," he said. "What does it mean?"

Alexei held up a hand. "Before we get into that, there's something else I need to come forward about. Something I should've fessed up to quite a long time ago. My wife is a reporter."

"A... *what*?" Blackforest growled.

"And you withheld this?!" Miloje demanded, mustache twitching with fury. "For the *months* that you've been married!? Irresponsible! Unconscionable! This is an outrage!"

"I know," Alexei admitted, hanging his head. "And believe me, I've lived for little more than to regret it. But you see, I *had* to tell you, now. For this is precisely what they meant to leverage against me." He gestured at the envelope in Horus' hand.

Horus looked on it with fresh amazement. "What did they want in return for their silence?"

"Only money," Alexei replied. "That's all the Maw of the Chantrieri hungers for."

"But it's impossible," Miloje said. "The seal is a forgery. It can't be the same Maw. Their master is dead. The Inquisitors made sure of it."

The Captain shook his head. "I understand better than any how impossible it seems. I watched them clear her hoard myself. The Inquisitors aren't merely adept at spying out treasure. They can *smell* it. I'm certain they couldn't have overlooked anything in their cunning."

"You mean," Horus was forced to conclude, "the orchestrator of this blackmail ring is a *dragon*?"

"*Was*," Miloje insisted. "Her name was Nayapaishira – a Pirate Lord who had the pluck to try to hide in plain sight – not over distant seas but imbedded right *here*, at the southern end of the civilized world. But as I say: she's dead."

"But how can you be absolutely *sure*?" Horus argued. "What about the dragon attack earlier this very week? Who's to say it wasn't this 'Nayapaishira' herself?"

"It doesn't fit the MO of a Pirate Lord, Mr. Templar, Sir," Alexei explained. "They've all the wickedness of a feral dragon, but they're infinitely more clever… and cowardly. They recruit their pirate bands to accept all the risk for them while they reap the lion's share of the rewards."

"Never mind that the Pirate Lord in question is *dead*," Miloje went on ad nauseum.

"What difference does it make?" Blackforest cut back in. "Real Maw or no – real Nayapaishira or no – we have the same problem. Someone's just attempted to blackmail one of our Captains with a closely-guarded secret."

"I *wish* that was our problem, Mr. Blackforest, Sir," Alexei said. "The long and short of it, I mean. But what are the chances this only goes as far as me? Not good. Not good at all. There's no telling how many secrets they already have, and mean to cash in on. No way of knowing how many more of those black envelopes are waiting to be delivered."

"Or already have been," Blackforest completed the thought, rubbing the back of his neck. "I see what you meant when you brought us here, Alexei. It's not a question of one mole anymore. We could be up against a hundred."

Horus eyed Alexei intently. "Would it really come to that? Would they compel officers of the law to be spies for them? To act in their interests? You said they only asked you for money."

"Money is their object – make no mistake. And that's what they lead with. But the first payment only confirms that the victim has a secret he means to keep at all costs. There's no telling what they'll ask of him next. Favors; information. Once they know they can leverage you, they'll turn a profit any way they can."

No one had anything more to say for a while after that.

"And we thought we were in a bind before," Miloje lamented, kneading his bobby. "An army of Jamisons couldn't help us now."

"But a bit of honesty might," Horus suggested. "Alexei exposed his own dark secret, rather than let himself be manipulated. I don't doubt the balance of the St. Argonsburg Police Department shares his virtue."

"That's a fine sentiment, Horus," Blackforest replied. "But all it takes is one bad egg in the bunch. One snitch, and we might never pull this thorn out of our side. I don't like our prospects."

Again, the room fell silent.

"Well, what say we act on what we know?" Miloje came around to suggesting. "All agreed that Bishop Sabracore needs censuring. A matter like that shouldn't wait."

"Yes," Blackforest agreed. "You're right, Stenya. Fortunately, I think I have something in mind for him."

He led the Deputy Constable out. Art wandered along with them, not appearing to notice Horus and Alexei lagging behind. Horus watched his friend go, seeing disconnect written all over him. Throughout their entire counsel in Alexei's office, he'd had no input. Likely as not, eavesdropping on Sabracore's punishment was his only remaining interest in the matter. Horus had many causes for concern. But he'd also emerged with one small joy that gave him hope...

"I'm very sorry, Mr. Templar," Alexei said, when the two of them were the only ones left in his office. "You cautioned me not to keep it a secret. I even went so far as to tell you I wouldn't. But I did, just the same."

"Yes, you did," Horus replied, making Alexei slump. But he reached out and put his hand on the Captain's shoulder. "But when the chips were down, you made the right choice. You're a leader here, Alexei – in rank, and in spirit. The department will withstand its trials yet, if they follow your example."

With a pat and a grin, Horus ambled out of the room.

Bereft of witnesses, Alexei permitted himself a rather silly smile. "A leader – in rank and in spirit." Finally, he began to follow the rest. "Perhaps the stringy little boy from Podunkville is doing alright for himself, after all."

Chapter 17

The night was dismal, and the morning brought no cheer. Horus and Deborah met dutifully by the train station. It was still an awful mess. For a little while, they just stood there, watching – hands mostly buried in pockets against the unseasonably cold morning – as armies of beleaguered railway workers went on trying to sort out rank upon rank of valence cars. After what felt like an hour of no discernible change, Horus led them away without so much as a word. And in that spirit, they continued on for some time, deep into the city.

"So..." Deborah abruptly segued into their long silence. "What's on your mind, Boss?"

Naturally, she wouldn't choose the best time to ask such a question. "Are you sure you want to talk about it? You might not be very impressed with the answer."

"It might be better for *both* of us to talk more, and think less."

"Alright. I was still thinking about Adam."

She sighed. "I guess I shouldn't wonder. What about him? I thought you resigned yourself to the fact he got away."

"I can't accept that," he stated.

"Well, then, turn it over to Blackforest. Tell him what you know, and he can tail Adam. Obviously, he means to go on jaywalking."

Horus shook his head. "It just rings off-key. I suppose I *could* breach his confidence, now. There are plenty of reasons I *should*. But I can't bring myself to feel good about simply handing him over to the hounds, either. I keep thinking about Khonshu... what a mess that was. And yet it all turned out right, in the end. I represented him the best I could. But even after I ultimately failed to defend him in court, I still got to make a second chance for him. There was hope. The possibility of redemption. This couldn't be more the opposite." He was quietly thoughtful for a moment. "It's just such a thorn. I never imagined Adam did it, because it didn't seem he *could*. Even now, I can't help wondering how he did it. Perhaps if I could only push past *that* distraction, a solution to all this would present itself."

"You certainly invest a lot of yourself in your clients. Even the worst ones."

"Maybe it's just easier right now," Horus said with a half-shrug. "Easier than trying to sort out other matters more pressing."

Deborah, of course, was more minded to think on those pressing matters. "I wonder where Art is right now. What he's up to."

"I'm confident we'll see him when we get where we're going."

She questioned him with her eyes. "Where *are* we going?"

"A burial."

"Detective Jamison?"

He shook his head. "No. A *live* burial."

* * *

With a great heave, the huge cement block buckled the plywood shelf they'd thrown over the old cistern. Every time the big, sweaty policemen added a new weight to the shelf, they held their breath, fearing that the structure might collapse then and there. Finally, the creak, the bounce, and the low sag of the plywood were such that they knew the boards would bear no more.

"Careful, my *child*," the Bishop chuckled above them, bound tightly in chains to the massive weights. "We wouldn't want to cut the festivities short, now, would we?"

"You won't be laughing in a minute, when your only 'children' are the darkness and the silence," Blackforest snarled. "There won't be any mind games left to play where you're going."

"Then perhaps now's as good a time as any for one more," Sabracore replied. "You think you've outsmarted me by casting me off. But consider this: Maybe you're still doing *exactly* what I intended you to do. Maybe you have been all along."

"That's a chance I'm willing to take." Blackforest turned to the town crier. "Read the charges."

The man dutifully unrolled and read the scroll in his hands. "Bishop Sabracore: you float accused of Criminal Conspiracy and Unrepentant Heresy, for which the previously prescribed penalty of life imprisonment has proven grossly inadequate. You are thereby sentenced to be flung to the watery depths and buried alive. May the Creators have mercy on your soul."

"So be it," Sabracore assented, unafraid. "I say plant a seed of truth and watch it grow."

Blackforest instructed the policemen with a gesture. "Do it."

They pulled the plywood slabs out from under the burden like so much tablecloth, and Sabracore's weights drew him down in a flash. All gathered for the proceedings listened breathlessly. But such was the depth of the old well that they never even heard the splashdown at the bottom. It was altogether uncanny.

"...I'm not at all sure I wanted to see that," Deborah remarked quietly to Horus, at length.

"I'm sorry. It *was* a frightfully unpleasant matter. But the Bishop's end demanded witnesses. And the more, the better."

"Didn't you say Art was going to be here?" she asked.

"Yes. If anyone had a reason to see this, it was him."

"Well, I think he missed it, Horus."

Horus looked up, scanning the crowd. She was right. He wasn't anywhere to be seen. "That's... rather alarming," he said, feeling even worse than he let on.

"Maybe he decided he'd already seen quite enough of Sabracore," she tried. "Maybe he's content to read about it in the papers. Assuming this makes it to print, that is."

"I hope that's all it is." He turned to her. "Or better yet: that his work was proscriptive."

* * *

As a matter of fact, at that very moment, Art was knocking on the front door of a former business associate. The man was soon to regret being so quick to answer, when he saw who it was on his front porch...

"*Y-you*?" T.R. Winnebaker asked, too unpleasantly surprised to stop himself. "Wh...what are you doing here?" He looked Art up and down. "You're not still my editor, are you?"

"Nope. I can happily say I never have ta touch that garbage you write again as long as I live."

Winnebaker waited what felt like a long time for something more. "Okay?"

"But ya know what? It's no good anyway. I've got your story stuck in my brain now – just like a bad song. It's been annoying the living daylights outta me for what already feels like forever. So much so that I had ta come down here and hassle ya about it."

"...Alright...?"

"So your main characters – Mark and Holly – they almost got engaged, right?"

"Yeah."

"That was your first stupid mistake. Why in the Undervoid would two *Humans* meet, date, and get engaged? That's not how it works for you people!"

"But... it's a fantasy story," Winnebaker explained. "Things are supposed to be a little different. It's called 'suspension of disbelief'."

"Yeah, well, that's a pretty tall order, Bub. But anyway, I digress. Here's what's really tickin' me off. Holly split ta go pursue her dream job in some dumb place called... 'Cleveland'... or something. Right?"

"Right."

"And Mark got caught in that lodge they saved together under a 3000-foot-deep avalanche. Right?"

"Right."

"Okay, so tell me this: How is it supposed ta work out for them in the end? *How*?"

"I... I don't know," Winnebaker despaired. "I haven't figured that part out yet."

"But they *are* gonna work it out? Aren't they?"

"Well... yes. I mean, of course! What's the point of telling a story like that if they didn't?"

Art folded his arms. "Now there's the million-dollar-question, Mac."

Winnebaker shook his head. "What do you mean? I don't understand."

"Well, did ya ever think there might be people out there in the world that it's *not* working out for? People who might be just the *teensiest* bit interested ta know what the Heck we're supposed to go do with ourselves now that it's not? Ya ever think about *that*? Well? Did ya!?"

"What do you want from me?" Winnebaker fired back, driven to the point of total exasperation. "I...I'm just a writer! I've never been married. Obviously I've never dated. What would I know about it?!"

Art scoffed. "Yeah. What *would* you know about it?"

He walked away, leaving behind a shell-shocked young author, who watched him go with wondering eyes.

The whole visit had been a complete waste of his time.

Just as he knew it would be.

"*Fantasy writers...*" Art muttered under his breath.

* * *

Later that same day, Horus found himself making a domestic visit to a former business associate of his own. When he'd signaled his presence by rapping on the door, he had time to second-guess himself. There were two people who might answer, and he rather dreaded to see either one of them. One would be only too happy to sense his drear, and do what she could to magnify it. The other would surely try to make him feel better, which – if unsuccessful – might ultimately be worse. But of course, there was nowhere else he wanted to be right now anyway. That thought alone was enough to keep him at the door, until it opened...

"Oh. Hello, Counselor," Doctor Nokkaeru greeted him quietly. Naturally, it would be her, and not her husband.

"Doctor," he replied.

"I am most surprised to see you. To what do I attribute this house call you're making?"

"Well..." With his gear waiting in a cart behind him, he rubbed the back of his neck. "Of course, I never finished the work on your wall. And I left the floor a horrible mess. It seemed to me that – while I'm between cases – I ought to make it right."

She was dumbstruck. "That's... very kind. But really, it's none of your concern any longer."

"I hope you'll let me fix it, just the same."

The Doctor hesitated again. "May I ask why?"

He searched for a likely excuse. Unfortunately, all he could arrive at was tender honesty. "There's a lot going on right now that I haven't found an answer for. I'm just trying to focus on righting whatever wrongs I can."

At this point, he would've expected her to laugh at him, or make some other sign of fiendish amusement. But instead, she nodded solemnly. "I understand. Please, come in."

Horus added his can of paint-thinner to the lineup, intending to start with his damage to the floor. He was dimly aware that going back to the walls later would more than likely result in at least a few more spots on the ground. He didn't really care if he had to repeat some of the work.

"It's rather a shame your accomplice couldn't be here to help clean up," Nokkaeru said, delight at his expense still strangely absent from her voice.

"Oh? Where is Forasius? Working, I suppose."

"No indeed. Even as we speak, he is returning home."

The news fairly struck him in the gut. Another senseless parting. Another bad end. "I'm very sorry to hear that. Of course, we didn't know each other long, but I considered him a friend. I'm honestly rather surprised he would leave without first exchanging farewells."

"Forasius has many, many... *many* words, it is true. But when it comes to goodbyes, he has never been eloquent. I am sure he wishes you well, Counselor."

"Thank you. I hope you'll convey my best wishes." He felt another pang. "That is, if the two of you ever correspond."

She nodded. "We shall."

Horus was pleasantly surprised that she seemed earnestly intent to speak with her own husband again at some point. It was more than he expected from her. But then, she seemed very off today on the whole. Subdued. Almost agreeable...

"How is our mutual friend, the Investigator?" she suddenly asked, quashing his momentary good feeling.

"Not at all well, last I knew," he admitted.

She hung her head. "He expressed great sorrow to me at our last meeting. I fear my response was received as rather tactless."

Horus blanched, imagining the general drift of that conversation. "I can't imagine."

"I've thought often about what he said. About the grief he must have felt to so rebuke me." She turned her gaze back up to him, a question in her goggles. "Is it quite warped, Counselor, that I should find no solace in the misery of a friend?"

"Not at all. In fact, quite the contrary: I'd say that's the most normal feeling you've ever expressed."

She looked down again. "You should know: Such has been the depth of my reflection that I have lately changed my mind... in a most significant way." She took a moment to wind herself up to the admission. "I too will be returning to my homeland. I have sought authorization, which of course is but a formality, since Forasius already had it arranged that I should return if I wished. My transfer orders will not be long delayed."

Horus couldn't suppress his elation at the news. "You're leaving?" he asked with a smile. Doctor... this is extraordinary."

"I thought you would be well pleased. But of course, this isn't to humor *you*. It's not on account of your absurd counseling, either. It is at the admonishment of Mallard alone that I reached this decision. Let there be no mistake about that."

"Well, I think you've made the right choice, in any case," he replied, not at all abashed. "I know Forasius will think so." He shook his head, warm with disbelief. "I'm not sure you can appreciate how timely this is. To know that at least one of us has a happy future in store."

"I suppose, inevitably, there will be *some* joy," she lamented. "But whatever else may change, I will never be cheerful. I never was, nor do I ever wish to be."

"If that's what makes you happy, Doctor," Horus teased her. "When will you be going? But I suppose you wouldn't know yet."

"I hope to return in time for Forasius to present his paper on bilateral asymmetry. That will be a good surprise for him – alas – but at least I will be there to flaunt his brilliance. It is among his few redeeming qualities."

"He told me a bit about the paper. All the strange ways that people aren't as perfectly mirrored from left to right as they seem."

"I do hope he didn't prattle on endlessly about the menagerie of peculiar defects he's researched," she sighed. "Hands attached backwards; extra digits; stunted growth. The body can break its blueprint in oh so many ways..."

Horus was caught up suddenly in a flashing montage of memories. A whole host of them broke on his consciousness in brief, concentrated bursts. Adam lifting his big left foot out of its shoe; revealing his battered eye... the way he stumbled down the stairs the very first time they met... the little comment Blucille made when they were all dancing...

"By Carlos, I think I have it," he muttered to himself. He shook loose from his daze to regard Nokkaeru. "Doctor, have you ever heard of a case of...?"

"Dwarfism in Bilateral Sinesterpodia?" she rapidly interrupted. "It is *well* within the realm of possibility."

He dropped his brush and leapt for the door. "I have to go," he explained. At the threshold, though, he paused, casting guilty looks around the atrocious floor. "I hope you don't mind my abandoning the effort for the time being."

"Counselor Templar, remember that I will not be residing here much longer," she reminded him. "If this mess falls to someone else, it would only serve to amuse me. For goodness' sake, fly!"

* * *

That night enjoyed the good fortune of being particularly dark and unwholesome – just the sort of night that any self-respecting, unironic villain would feel compelled to make the most of. The sky was thick and stifling – utterly black, as if the very deepest depth of the void was hovering just overhead. The streets were quiet as the grave. Anyone who had the luxury was trying to sleep off their travails, and their malaise. The city, of course, was never *completely* at rest. But here, in a disused corner of old-town, what life was left had a penchant for making itself scarce. Adam Oppenheimer would've had to admit he'd played it safe, choosing this humble borough to restart his reign of terror. No matter. What he left behind tonight would be found sooner or later, just as it always had been before. He could dare more populous locales later on. The principal thing was, he couldn't let it rest. Jaywalking was a mission. A creed. A consuming hunger. Jaywalking was life. It was high time he got back to living it...

But just as he squared up with an empty crosswalk, he heard something stir up ahead – the sound of tiny feet coming his way. With both eyes uncovered, and wide with sudden alarm, he watched a shadow start to take shape in the gloom. And at last, to his surprise – and great relief – Horus Templar stepped into the meager light of an anemic streetlamp.

"Well, well, well," Adam called out. "I guess it's just like they say. For every Whiffle you shake off, another rises to take his place. Are you really the kind of man to hold a grudge, Horus? I'd say we did alright by each other, all things considered. Why not let it go?"

"I can't do that, Adam," Horus replied, holding his ground at the far side of the crosswalk. "Certainly not without a few parting words of wisdom." He looked indignantly down at the street between them, then back up. "I see you're intent to squander the gift you've been given at the first opportunity. But maybe you haven't stopped to consider what your acquittal could mean for you."

"And what might that be?"

"Only the most precious thing of all. A second chance."

Adam laughed. "You really think you're going to stand there, deliver some Indigo Scout speech and get me to turn over a new leaf? Just like that?"

"I think it's worth trying. Can't you see, Adam? This really could be the start of a new and better life for you. You should've paid for your crimes... but you got away instead. Why not let Left-Foot Lazarus perish, as he was meant to? Why not live out the life you've been granted in good faith, as Adam Oppenheimer?"

"Wow," Adam said, staring at Horus with raised brows. "A genuine appeal to my finer virtues. As if I had any. Come on, Horus. I thought we understood each other."

"Well, if you won't be moved by virtue, at least consider the pragmatic side of things," Horus insisted. "You know they're going to catch up with you eventually. The sooner now – I'm sure – that you've come under suspicion once before."

"I can't really fight you on that one," Adam sighed, stroking his chin. "But you know, I've been doing some thinking. There's really nothing to tie me down here. Figure maybe I could leave a few more prints around St. Argonsburg and move on to exciting new frontiers. I have to say, the rumors coming out of Maenea these days are just scrumptious. Sounds like it's shaping up to be just the kind of place where my way of looking at the world could really take root." He winked his crimson eye, then took his first few steps out into the street. "Besides, if I turn back now, you'd always be left *wondering*. You'd never get to see how it's done."

"I already know how you do it," Horus revealed.

This information froze Adam in his tracks. "You do?"

"I do." He pointed down at Adam's feet. "Blucille Cordon was right on the nose that night, though she didn't know it. None of us did at the time. But who would ever dream it was true? Who would think to blame your clumsy streak on a literal occurrence of a whimsical expression? Who – when presented with your enormous left foot – would demand to see the other one, as well? The other *left* foot, that is. The one on the end of your right leg."

Adam pursed his lips – let out a slow breath through his nose. "Well, look at you. So much more clever than I gave you credit. You're exactly right, Horus." He leaned down, helping himself out of the size 13 shoe on his right. Even knowing what to expect, Horus found the unearthly sight of the small, left-facing shoe underneath it turned his stomach as it came to rest beside its larger counterpart on the ground. A silty scent drifted to him from the exposed sole. Adam straightened back up. "The shoe is on the other foot."

"Alright. Now we've had an end to the mystery. Let it rest, Adam. You don't have to follow through with this."

"But I do." He started walking again. "Don't you see it now, Horus? It's the way I'm built. This is what I was *made* for. It's my destiny."

Horus shook his head. "You can't believe that. You can't believe you were made to do this evil thing."

"Define evil. If the Creators had any strongly held notion of right and wrong, they should've stuck around to enforce it." He slowly began to drift to the left as he made his march, carrying the weight of fate with every purposeful stride. "You know what I think? I think 'morality' comes down to one simple maxim. Either they get what they want, or I do. I choose me."

Horus held his hand out. "I'm warning you. Don't. Don't take that step."

"Just watch me."

Adam veered right past the white boundary, taking *two* steps out – a wide one with the left leg to make room for the right, so that the dirty shoe left its wayward mark. He smiled, clearly assuming Horus hadn't reasoned out all the finest choreographic points of committing the crime. "How do you like that, Horus? I was always further out of line than it seemed."

Horus sighed, defeated. "Yes, you were. And now, you'll pay the price."

Adam flinched as he began to hear other footsteps converging in the darkness. His eyes darted wildly. A whole contingent of police officers emerged from nearby alleys all throughout his field of vision. He whirled around, but found his retreat was cut off. Finally, he watched as the Deputy Constable and the District Attorney drew up beside Horus – his betrayer.

Caught, with no hope of escape, Adam's look of feral fright slowly gave way to his ire. "So that's how it is, huh?" he asked Horus. "I admit: I didn't think you had it in you to sell me out. I thought you had principles."

"I asked these men to follow me," Horus explained. "I didn't say why. I told you not to do it. I *warned* you. I gave you every chance. They would've had nothing if you'd simply refrained. My conscience is clear. You didn't stumble into this one, Adam. You walked right into it."

Blackforest pointed lazily into the street. "Book him."

The officers rushed in and took hold of Adam by both arms, commencing to lead him away. But just as they reached Horus, Adam dug in, and they permitted the exchange he obviously meant to have.

For a moment, Adam said nothing. He only studied Horus… before an ugly smile returned to his ghastly face. "You *still* feel sorry for me, don't you? After everything I said. Everything I've done. You still hate to see it end this way."

Horus only stared back. There didn't seem anything fitting to say in return.

Seeing there would be no more words, the cops got around to carrying Adam off. He cast a final look of amusement over his shoulder, just as he and his escorts disappeared into the shadows.

Horus exchanged cheerless glances with Miloje and Blackforest, before they too turned to go, leaving him alone on the edge of the street. At length, he wandered off himself, as the last rumor of their footsteps regressed, and the silence of the night closed in. He only wished he could hear it. He wished for any sound at all beside the one he fancied that he heard...

It was the faint echo of the dragon's dying cry.

Acknowledgments

Many thanks to Josh, who really encouraged me, and helped me give some life to characters who would otherwise have been flat. Thanks to Gilbert, who came up with Eleven Christopher Snorkel, whether he remembers it or not, dang it. I'm much indebted to Lee, who gifted me the train-hopping idea that made the middle of the book finally possible. Many thanks to my grandma, who went out of her way time and again to do whatever she could to encourage my progress in this book. Thanks to John for putting some really choice medical jargon in my reach, and to Rebekka for at least one especially great plot twist she inspired. To my mom, who I know did all she could to help out, and caught many key errors, as always! To Ben: I couldn't have done it without your knowing about your neighbors' totally sweet landscaping! And to your neighbors, Tom and Karen: Thank you ever so much for letting me take a picture of your pavement, without which I would be sunk! Finally, thanks to Coleman – for something, I guess.

For More from E.L. Ward...

Visit his personal site, at:

https://www.booksofelward.com

His vast arsenal of backlist titles includes the following:

TITLES IN THE ORPHAN UNIVERSE

HERON PROPHECIES SERIES

The Chocolate Prophecy

HORUS TEMPLAR – PUBLIC DEFENDER SERIES

Horus Templar and the Case of the Wimpy War-Criminal
Horus Templar and the Case of the Iniquitous Inquisitor
Horus Templar and the Case of the Draft-Dodging Drone
Horus Templar and the Case of the Dubious Decedent
Horus Templar and the Case of the Vengeful Vigilant
Horus Templar and the Case of the Jolly Jaywalker

E.L. Ward is proud to partner with:

MALOB ARTS

MALO
MOSTLY A LOT OF BOZOS
ARTS

Check out his and other creative works at:

www.malobarts.com

Made in the USA
Monee, IL
04 November 2026

67386550R00108